Using ICT
in the Early Years

Parents and practitioners in partnership

Revised and updated

by Alex Morgan and John Siraj-Blatchford

Woodbury Centre

Published by Practical Pre-School Books, A Division of MA Education, St Jude's Church, Dulwich Road, Herne Hill, London, SE24 0PB.
Tel: 020 7738 5454   www.practicalpreschoolbooks.com

© MA Education 2009. This edition printed 2013.

Illustrations by Cathy Hughes. Front cover images main image © iStockphoto.com/Mokai. Smaller images (left to right) © Petro Feketa/Fotolia, © iStockphoto.com/FhaSud, © MA Education photo taken by Ben Suri. Back cover images (left to right): © Olesiabilkei/Fotolia, © MA Education photo taken by Lucie Carlier.

ISBN 978-1-909280-57-1

Please note that all websites and reference works cited were accessible and available at the time of going to press. Unfortunately, owing to the ever-changing nature of the Internet please be aware that website addresses may well vary from those cited in this book.

Acknowledgements

Acknowledgement is due to colleagues at Thomas Coram, Homerton and Gamesley Nursery schools. To Pamela Attmore, Judy Norton and Mary Carnell in Cambridgeshire, Kimberly Smith in Leeds, and Kate Wilde, Chrissie Dale, Marie Folland, and Julie Oxlade in Northamptonshire. To Jan Morgan, Louisa Reynolds-Milnes, the teachers who worked so hard with us on the 'Supporting Playful learning with ICT in the Early Years project' as well as countless other practitioners who have shared their examples of good practice with us over the years.

Introduction

This book provides guidance and illustrations of good practice to support all those working with young children (teachers, nursery nurses, childminders and other early years educators) and their families, in applying a range of Information and Communications Technologies (ICTs) to support early learning. The text was originally written to support a Randomised Controlled Trial of a complex intervention – using ICT to support adult-child interactions in the home learning environment (HLE) with children aged 3-4 years over a one-year period which aimed to improve their cognitive and linguistic outcomes. Findings indicate the intervention had a significant effect on children's phonological awareness and early numerical concepts. This provides clear evidence to support the idea that when ICT tools are used specifically to support, develop and extend adult-child interactions there may be cognitive and linguistic benefits for young children.

This second edition has been improved by what has been learnt from the project through feedback from parents and practitioners and analysis of adult-child interactions with ICT. It has also been extended to include more examples of sustained shared thinking with ICT and also novel concepts and ideas. The concepts of dialogic reading and print referencing also have a robust research base and the potential to further enhance the learning experiences pre-school children have in the HLE with ICT.

The sections are organised in terms of rationale, including a programme of practical activities, an index and technical glossary that are provided to support its ongoing use as a source of reference.

The aim of this publication is to support parents and professionals working together in the application of ICT in early childhood and this particular approach has been adopted for two reasons. Most importantly, the approach acknowledges the growing efforts being made by parents to provide for children's early learning with ICT in the home. It also recognises the major contribution that can be made to early childhood education by early years settings in their application of appropriate ICTs within their settings, and through their partnership with parents and families.

The growth and effects of ICT use in the home

The number and the range of ICTs that have been introduced into the home has massively increased in recent years and a significant proportion of this new technology has been purchased specifically for use by young children. Industry sources suggest that the total global market for educational toys was $2.1 billion in 2006 and this is expected to grow to $7.3 billion by 2011[1]. In both the UK and the USA, computer software aimed at the youngest children also constitutes the fastest growing segment of the overall youth software market[2]. These market growth statistics have run counter

to many other industrial trends, with the growth being maintained despite a global economic recession. In part, this may be explained and considered a reflection of the fact that parental aspirations for their children have been rising. This has been a trend identified in national surveys. Parents have higher educational expectations for their children, and one way in which they have been concerned in supporting their children's early learning has been through ICT. Young children are therefore gaining access to more ICT. But not all observers have seen this as a positive development.

Almost every day there is a newspaper headline relating to the dangers 'new technologies' pose for young children. Recently a pscycologist, Aric Sigman stated that he believed that screens should be banned for children under the age of nine[3]. This case against ICT in early childhood has been made in terms of the perceived risks to children's physical, cognitive and emotional and social development[4]. Critics refer to possible repetitive strain injuries, a lack of exercise and risk of obesity, decreased creativity, impaired language and literacy, poor concentration, social isolation, decreased motivation and depression[5]. Yet the market statistics suggest that these arguments have had little influence on many parents and a number of studies have also shown that ICT, when used responsibly, can actually support children's learning; by offering children opportunities for more active learning of a wide range of skills, knowledge and competencies. Studies have shown benefits in the areas of fine motor skills, language and communication, emergent literacy and reading readiness, mathematical thinking, creativity, problem solving, self-esteem and self-confidence, cooperation, motivation, and positive attitudes towards learning[6].

Throughout the UK, greater emphasis has been placed on the importance of the outdoor learning environment for young children and this is sometimes presented as compensation for 'toxic' influences upon early childhood that include ICT[7]. It is even suggested at times that ICT and outdoor play, may in some fundamental sense, be logically inconsistent. Yet such a case could only really be argued if one were to first assume that all ICTs were associated with desktop computers. This is demonstrably not the case. As adults we interact with a wide range of ICTs outdoors, and many of these may be applied for educational purposes. Laptop computers and tablet PCs with wireless connections are routinely used for a range of purposes in the outdoors. The use of satellite navigation and global positioning systems (GPS) have become commonplace in recent years. Metal detectors, traffic lights and mobile telephones provide additional examples of ICTs that have been applied effectively in a range of preschool settings. There is a good deal of scope for the integration of ICT in young children's

outdoor play environments. In fact, ICT is as much part of children's world (indoors and outdoors) as literacy and numeracy, or indeed any other feature of the complex worlds in which we live and struggle to make sense of.

ICT in outdoor play

On a visit to a Forest School in the South West of England, an enthusiastic environmental studies educator was extolling the benefits of the children learning in the outdoor environment. ICT was presented as a negative influence upon the children that had to be explicitly countered by involving them in more outdoor activities. At just that point a child came up to the educator to show them a particularly glossy dark green leaf that they had found. The educator admired the child's find, and suggested she look for some more so that she could take them back to the classroom and "make a mobile". To this the child's eyes lit up and she immediately put the leaf to her ear and said; "Hello Mum....". Later the children were showing off the 'dens' that they had improvised using sticks and undergrowth. Several children referred to the ICT features that they had incorporated into their play dens as 'doorbells', 'the TV' and 'video recorders' and so on. This case shows that, even when you deny children all

Introduction

access to ICT in the teaching and learning environment, they will still bring ICTs along with them in their fantasy play. Our choice as educators is not whether we are to include or to exclude ICT in early childhood education. Children will learn all sorts of things about ICT without our influence. The only choice that we have is whether we are to provide a critical ICT education or not. It makes no sense to pretend it isn't an influence on children, we can either leave children to learn about ICT uncritically from other sources, or we can accept the challenge of ICT and make the most of the opportunities that it offers.

Whilst there is some evidence of a relationship between the excessive and sedentary computer use of some older children, and their health problems related to inactivity, parents are generally reporting that children are leading active, well-balanced lives in which physical activity is not displaced by the use of ICT. Indeed, recent research on the role of ICT in children's lives indicates that parents are generally supportive of children's use of technology and that there is little evidence to suggest that it is detrimental to interactions in educational settings or to family life[8].

Yet special caution should be taken in early childhood when children are at their most vulnerable, and in the absence of any large-scale studies relating the use

of desktop computers to specific health indicators in young children, it makes sense to look at the evidence related to the use of any similar ICT in making any final judgements. Important lessons may be learnt from considering the research that has been conducted concerning television viewing. In the early days of television similar fears were expressed over its potentially harmful influence on children, and similar claims were also made for its powerful educational potential.

Research conducted in the past decade does provide evidence of television viewing impacting negatively upon many children's cognitive and academic achievement. The American Academy of Paediatrics recommends a maximum of one to two screen hours per child per day – including television and video – with less for pre-schoolers. Studies have found that children who watch television for less than one hour per day are more likely to obtain post-school qualifications including university degrees. A major study of 1,278 children at age one and three years found that 10% had attention problems at age seven. These children were watching an average of 2.2 hours of television per day at age one, and 3.6 hours at age three[9]. Another study of 8,400 seven-year-olds, carried out by Glasgow University, suggested that three-year old children who watch television for more than eight hours a week, are at greater risk of being obese by the age of seven and of remaining fat for the rest of their lives[10]. There are also studies that show the negative effects upon children of their parent's excessive television viewing. However, research also shows that some television programs, which have been specifically developed for young children, have positive effects. It also shows that where parents take a special interest in children's television, and they watch programmes together, children tend to watch less television, and they gain more from the experience. Specific television programmes have also been found to be effective in providing family support[11].

The key lesson to be learnt from the case of television is that where there have been problems, they have not been the result of the media or the technology itself, but the way in which it is sometimes misapplied. Young children sometimes view inappropriate programmes after the nine o'clock watershed and/or have access to inappropriate video material. These are potential problems that parents (and children) should be aware of and that professional educators and advocates for young children have a responsibility to address as well. In doing so we shouldn't forget that ICTs, including television, can (and often are) applied for positive ends, and that they provide significant support for children's early learning.

What the example of television highlights is the importance of all those who work with young children being aware of the potential risks, and for them to learn

how to make the most of the technology available to support children's early learning with and about ICT.

There are already studies that have investigated the use of computers by young children that suggest similar patterns of misuse in a minority of cases. Research shows that children from disadvantaged families are more likely to use computers at an early age, but that this use is often restricted to games software which provides minimal learning opportunities. At times the software may also be unsuitable. As the recently completed Byron Review[12] suggests, young children are particularly vulnerable in terms of content that is violent, frightening, sexual or highly emotional. Where the use of ICTs are regarded as a social activity and exposure to unsuitable content (on or off-line) can be monitored, avoided or discussed, then its learning potential may be maximised. A number of studies have found that the children of middle-class families tend to use home computers more often for educational purposes. However, the degree of ICT competence children acquire in the home clearly depends on a number of factors including: access to hardware, the support available for learning how to use the ICT, and the particular interests and aptitudes of older family members[13].

At the end of the day, the increased use of ICTs in the home may be considered a threat or a challenge. But whatever our thoughts on ICT are, we should recognise that ICTs aren't going to go away. ICT has significant potential to support learning, and it is essential that all of those concerned for young children's futures work together to minimise the negative impact and make the most of its potential.

has been developed for use by early years educators working with children that allow children to create and make changes in images, text and in the sound effects of their media products and stories. The approach that we are taking throughout the book is also grounded in four firmly established and evidence-based principles of good practice in early childhood education and in the next two chapters these ideas are explored in more detail:

1. Enhanced interaction, dialogue and 'sustained shared thinking' in early childhood have been identified as strongly associated with children's learning and development in the home and in preschool settings.

2. Young children have been shown to benefit significantly from enriched language environments. The use of specific strategies to develop metalinguistic awareness such as dialogic reading and print referencing have been shown to provide significant support pre-school children's emergent literacy.

3. Enriched Home Learning Environments (HLEs) in early childhood have been found to significantly contribute towards long-term educational achievement. Research has shown this to be true even where children are otherwise disadvantaged due to poverty, limited parental education, income or employment.

4. Developmentally appropriate software has been found to support the development of creativity, communication and collaboration in the early years.

Maximising the learning potential of ICT in early childhood

The quality of software currently available for early childhood education is extremely varied and much of it has been subjected to sustained criticism from those engaged in developing good practice. Most early years software, has been developed with the built-in assumption that the child will individually interact with the technology on their own. Yet, as we will show throughout this book, there are also many examples of software that may be applied to encourage adult-child and child-child communication, collaboration and creativity. There are adventure games and simulations that have been developed for older children to use on their own, that we have found both stimulating and highly motivating for younger children when used with adult support. There is also software available that

Creativity, communication and collaboration

A curriculum emphasis upon creativity, communication and collaboration has been identified as the most appropriate to prepare children for their future employment in our future knowledge-based societies. It is likely that in the workplace of the future key skills will include the ability to access and critically analyse information, as well as monitor and control their own learning. There is also general agreement among developmental psychologists and educationalists that creativity, communication and collaboration are all especially important in the early years. From the earliest stages of children's learning and development we know that when children share 'joint attention' in activities this process provides a significant cognitive challenge in itself. As children get older, collaboration

Introduction

is considered important in providing opportunities for cognitive conflict as they become aware of alternative understandings in their efforts to reach consensus with others. Collaboration also offers a possibility for the co-construction of potentially better solutions in creative and problem solving contexts. The major features of progression in terms of creativity, communication and collaboration have been identified as follows[14]:

1. The baby initially learns to manipulate signs (like eye contact and smiles) in their emotional communications with adults and peers, and they engage in significant gestures.
2. Pretend play and object substitution become internalised (as imagination) as they begin to have internal conversations or 'think to themselves' (i.e. to develop 'inner speech').
3. The child begins to use objects to symbolise things, and to use signs in their pretend play (a practice that may be initially introduced to the child by an adult or peer).
4. The child is first able to take on a 'role', then develops the capability of interacting with pretend others (increasingly acknowledging 'their' perspective), and then 'switches' freely between roles.
5. Role play becomes more collaborative as partners at first share symbols and then negotiate the roles that they adopt in their play with others.
6. Conceptual knowledge and understanding of the 'other' (ie of someone other than themselves) and of the 'self', develop further and particular 'dispositions' (positive and negative attitudes) towards learning various subjects become more significant.
7. Most children become motivated towards more formal learning and schooling.

Play and imitation provide primary contexts for representational and symbolic behaviour. Artefacts such as toys and other 'manipulables', such as wooden building blocks, are important because they provide symbols for the children to play with. The stack of blocks may become a castle or a tower, a single block may represent a car or an aeroplane. When children play with both functioning and pretend technological artefacts, such as telephones or photocopiers, they serve the same purpose: to act as 'props' in the children's play. Computer applications provide a means by which children may engage and interact with a much wider range of 'virtual' artefacts and environments than would otherwise be possible. The potential for such onscreen symbol manipulation using computers has long been recognised, and a wide range of existing software may be applied by adults to exploit this potential, even where it may be considered unsuitable for individualised play in early childhood. A good example might be for a parent to be playfully

creating images for a child using the Microsoft (MS) Paint program. A child under the age of two would gain little from this software on their own, but an adult can usefully create (or upload) images for them, and engage them in a conversation, verbal exchange (or dialogue) by manipulating the images (signs and symbols) on the screen. By manipulating the size, shape and position of the images the adult can enhance and sustain their dialogue with the child.

Dialogue and sustained shared thinking

One of the key findings of the Researching Effective Pedagogy in the Early Years (REPEY) project[15], a study closely related to, and building upon the EPPE study, was that adult-child interactions, that involved some element of 'sustained shared thinking' (SST), may be especially valuable to children's early learning. The REPEY project revealed a general pattern of better learning outcomes associated with sustained adult-child verbal interactions. SST is defined as **'an effective pedagogic interaction, where two or more individuals 'work together' in an intellectual way to solve a problem, clarify a concept, evaluate activities or extend a narrative'.** In SST both adult and child were found to contribute to the thinking, which was found to develop and extend.

The best examples of SST are by definition extended and this limits the possibility for illustration, but the following examples are usefully cited by Siraj-Blatchford (2009)[16]:

BOY 3 (3yrs, 11m, has finished his cake and starts to sing 'Happy Birthday' to NURSERY OFFICER 1.)
NURSERY OFFICER 1: (Pretends to blow out the candles.) Do I have a present?
BOY 3 hands her a ball of playdough.
NURSERY OFFICER 1: I wonder what's inside? I'll unwrap it. (She quickly makes the ball into a thumb pot and holds it out to BOY 3) It's empty!
BOY 3 (takes a pinch of playdough and drops it into the thumb pot.) It's an egg.
NURSERY OFFICER 1 (picking it out gingerly): It's a strange shape.
BOY 1 (4yrs, tries to take the 'egg'.)
NURSERY OFFICER 1: Be very, very careful. It's an egg. To BOY 3: What's it going to hatch into?
BOY 3: A lion.
NURSERY OFFICER 1: A lion? .... I can see why it might hatch into a lion, it's got little hairy bits on it. (She sends BOY 3 to put the egg somewhere safe to hatch. He takes the egg and goes into the bathroom.)
(Dialogue continues...)

CONTEXT: Children engaged in water play. BOY 8 (4yrs, 1m) (who has been watching various items floating on water): Look at the fir cone. There's bubbles of air coming out.

NURSERY OFFICER 1: It's spinning round.
BOY 8 (4yrs, 1m): That's 'cos it's got air in it.
NURSERY OFFICER 1: (picks up the fir cone and shows the CHILDREN how the scales go round the fir cone in a spiral, turning the fir cone round with a winding action), When the air comes out in bubbles it makes the fir cone spin around.
GIRL 2E (4yrs, 9m): (uses a plastic tube to blow into the water), Look bubbles.
NURSERY OFFICER 1: What are you putting into the water to make bubbles?...... What's coming out of the tube?
GIRL 2E (4yrs, 9m): Air.
(Dialogue continued…)

The nursery officer in this example is clearly encouraging the child's open play, entering into and extending the dialogue without dominating it. The following example is drawn from data collected in a recent study published in *EYE magazine* (January 2010).

CONTEXT: Teacher 1 and child 2 (3yrs) are playing together with an onscreen duck flight simulator (See page 26 for more information on this game).

CHILD 2: I have already been to the pond!
CHILD 2: There were no ducks there!
TEACHER 1: There were no ducks! Oh no! Where do you think they were?
CHILD 2: I went with my daddy!
TEACHER 1: Shall we try and make this duck fly?
CHILD 2: Yes
TEACHER 1: This is the duck that we are going to try and make fly. We can change what it looks like to make it fly.
CHILD 2: I want bigger legs! (Mouse used to adjust size)
TEACHER 1: What's happening to the ducks legs?
CHILD 2: They are growing!
TEACHER 1: Do you think they are long enough yet?
CHILD 2: No, they need to be bigger like my legs! (sticks leg out!)
TEACHER 1: Oh you want them to be as long as your legs!
CHILD 2: Yes, so they can run really fast like me!
TEACHER 1: What else would you like to change?
CHILD 2: I would like it to have a bigger beak.
TEACHER 1: What can you see is happening when you press the button?

CHILD 2: I can see it's growing!
TEACHER 1: How about the wings?
CHILD 1: Bigger! Let's make them bigger and longer arms! (sticks arms out wide, as though he is a duck)
TEACHER 1: How about the duck's tummy?
CHILD 2: I want it to be a bit more bigger.
TEACHER 2: What do you think will happen if it has a bigger tummy?
CHILD 2: It will feel poorly.
CHILD 2: Ooo it's not as big as my tummy!
CHILD 2: I want to make it's eyes bigger!
TEACHER 1: You would like to make the eyes bigger? Ooh this program doesn't let us change how big or small the eyes are. What do you think would happen if you did make the eyes bigger?
(Dialogue continues…)

Again, the children are given the freedom to explore and the teacher is playing alongside them, supporting and extending the dialogue. When children are encouraged to initiate discussion and to ask questions their capacity to learn is increased. Research has established that early literacy is stimulated through the extended conversations that often occur during practical activities. ICT provides

Introduction

an excellent context for this. Theorists have also argued that, since children as young as three can understand language about their own learning and will use it, educators should try to raise children's awareness of their own learning and themselves as learners. For example, parents and other early educators can draw attention to how a child has used a new skill, or combined different materials or techniques, and they can show their recognition of the fact that a child has shown concentration, perseverance or solved a problem.

Computers provide a means by which young children may be supported in their manipulation of symbols, and representations on the screen in a manner that allows them to distance themselves from, and explore the properties of, the objects that their symbols represent. Screen-based activities can therefore support the processes of verbal reflection and abstraction. This is a theme specifically in the US National Research Council's report 'Eager to Learn: Educating Our Preschoolers'[17]. The report strongly endorses the application of computers in early childhood:

Computers help even young children think about thinking, as early proponents suggested.[18]

In one study, preschoolers who used computers scored higher on measures of metacognition.[19]

Some strategies that parents and practitioners can use when they are engaging in sustained shared thinking in the context of ICT in the early years include:

- **Tuning-in:** listening carefully to what is being said, observing the child's body language and what they are doing.
- **Showing genuine interest:** giving their whole attention to the child, maintaining eye contact, affirming, smiling, nodding.
- **Respecting the children's own decisions and choices by inviting children to elaborate:** saying things like 'I really want to know more about this' and listening and engaging in the response.
- **Re-capping:** 'So you think that ... '
- **Offering the adult's own experience:** 'I like to listen to music when I cook supper at home.'
- **Clarifying ideas:** 'Right, Wayne, so you think that if we emptied the paintpot into this image it will escape through the gap?'
- **Suggesting:** 'You might like to try doing it this way.'
- **Reminding:** 'Don't forget that you said that the paint would spill out of the shape if there was a gap in the line.'
- **Using encouragement to further thinking:** 'You have really thought hard about where to put this door in the palace – where will you put the windows?'
- **Offering an alternative viewpoint:** 'What if the Big Bad Wolf was clever and he escaped because he could feel the heat of the fire coming up the chimney?'
- **Speculating:** 'What kind of house would you design to trick even the cleverest wolf?'
- **Reciprocating:** 'Thank goodness you saved your picture before the power went off Julie. I wasn't so careful the other day and I lost all of the reports that I had typed!'
- Using positive questioning
  - □ 'I don't know, what do you think?'
  - □ 'That's an interesting idea.'
  - □ 'I like what you have done there.'
  - □ 'Have you seen what X has done – why?'
  - □ 'I wondered why you had ... ?'
  - □ 'I've never thought about that before.'
  - □ 'You've really made me think.'
  - □ 'What would happen if we did ... ?'
- **Asking open questions:** 'What do you think?' 'I wonder what would happen if ... ?'
- **Modelling thinking:** 'I have to think hard about what I should do this lunch time. I need to phone the engineer because he has to come and fix the printer, I have to renew my library books on the Internet and I need to put out all the paints for the group this afternoon. But I just won't have time to do all of these things.'

There are some important hints and tips to consider when promoting SST with ICT in the early years:

- Ensure that the software supports communication, collaboration and creativity.
- Consider if there would be more dialogue between the adult and child if the adult has control of the

mouse or trackpad and the child has to instruct them when and where to click.

▨ Consider turning the sound off or intermittently use mute with some software to allow greater space for dialogue

▨ Encourage children to undertake an activity more than once engaging them in discussion regarding how they would like to change or develop their approach to the activity.

▨ Ensure that there are functional and pretend IT resources in the class themed role play area e.g. at the travel agent, at the vets.

[1] Cited in Wall, B. (2006) Ambitious parents spend on educational toys for toddlers. *International Herald Tribune:* Friday, November 24, 2006.

[2] Sandberg, J. (2000) Multimedia Childhood. *Newsweek* Your Child Issue, (Fall/Winter 2000).

[3] Clarke, L. (2010). Curse of the screen: PCs 'dull children's brains and should be banned until nine, Education Correspondent, Mail Online (http://www.dailymail.co.uk/health/article-1285981/TVs-PCs-dull-childrens-brains.html).

[4] Healy, M. J. (1999) *Failure to connect: How computers affect our children's minds and what we can do about it.* Simon and Schuster.

[5] Cordes, C., Miller, E., eds (2000) *Fool's gold: A critical look at computers in childhood,* Alliance for Childhood, College Park.

[6] Marsh, J., Brooks, G., Hughes, J. et al. (2005) *Digital Beginnings: Young People's Use of Popular Culture, Media and New Technologies.* University of Sheffield, Sheffield.

[7] Plowman, L., McPake, J., Stephen, C. (2008) The Technologisation of Childhood? Young Children, Technology and the Home. *Children and Society* (DOI:10.1111/j.1099-0860.2008.00180.x).

[8] Aubrey C, Dahl S (2008) *A review of the evidence on the use of ICT in the Early Years Foundation Stage.* Becta: Coventry.

[9] Christakis, D., Zimmerman, F., DiGiuseppe, D. et al. (2004) Early television exposure and subsequent attentional problems in children. *Pediatrics,* **113**: 708-714.

[10] Reilly, J., McDowell, Z. (2003b) Physical activity interventions in the prevention and treatment of paediatric obesity: systematic review and critical appraisal, Symposium on 'Physical activity, energy expenditure and obesity'. *Proceedings of the Nutrition Society* **62**: 611–19.

[11] Siraj-Blatchford, I. & Siraj-Blatchford, J. (2006) *A Guide to Developing the ICT Curriculum for Early Childhood Education.* Trentham Books, Stoke-on-Trent.

[12] *The Byron Review* (2008): http://www.dcsf.gov.uk/byronreview/ (accessed 22/9/9).

[13] McPake, J., Stephen, C., Plowman, L., Sime, D. et al. (2004) *Already at a Disadvantage? ICT in the Home and Children's Preparation for Primary School.* Becta, Coventry.

[14] Siraj-Blatchford, I. 'Creativity, Communication and Collaboration: The Identification of Pedagogic Progression in Sustained Shared Thinking'. Asia-Pacific. *Journal of Research in Early Childhood Education,* Vol. 1, No. 2, December 2007.

[15] Sylva, K., Melhuish, E., Siraj-Blatchford, I. et al. (2008) *The Effective Pre-School and Primary Education (EPPSE 3-11) project: final report.* DCSF: London.

[16] Siraj-Blatchford, I. (2009) Conceptualising progression in the pedagogy of play and sustained shared thinking in early childhood education: A Vygotskian perspective. *Educational and Child Psychology* 26 (2).

[17] Bowman, B., Donovan, S., Burns, S., eds (2001) *Eager to Learn: Educating our Preschoolers.* Commission of Behavioral Social Sciences and Education, National Research Council. National Academy Press: Washington DC.

[18] Papert, S. (1980). *Mindstorms: Children, Computers, and Powerful Ideas.* New York: Basic Books.

[19] Fletcher-Flinn, C. M. & Suddendorf, T. (1996). Do computers affect "the mind"?. *Journal of Educational Computing Research,* 15(2), pp. 97-112.

Role play

Role play provides powerful contexts for sustained shared thinking with, or without, ICT. ICT may be considered relevant to early education for two quite different reasons:

1. For the purposes of technology education
2. Its application in supporting children's learning across the curriculum.

Policies often emphasise the importance of ICT being applied to support children's learning across the curriculum, yet references are also frequently made to ICT being applied in a wider range of contexts wherever its use may be employed to demonstrate a common application of technology in the adult world (i.e. providing technology education). In role play it is often, but never entirely, technology education that is being prioritised. To take the example of the 'At The Vets' activity cited below, the children are able to apply the ICT to learn about the use of ICT in medical diagnosis (e.g. in creating an X-Ray) and also in accounting (making up the customer's bill). But in the process they also learn about some of the science applied in veterinary practice, about the use of numbers in accounting and about mark making in their record keeping.

Young children learn effectively not when they are merely told, but when they can shape their environment and construct knowledge for themselves through playful activity. Vygotsky highlighted this when he wrote that: *'in play the child is always behaving beyond his age, above his usual everyday behaviour; in play he is, as it were, a head above himself.'*[20]

But there are different kinds of play. Generally, children under the age of three engage in exploratory play. They observe, smell, taste, prod, taste, touch, push and pull whatever they encounter in order to learn about their world. We can enrich and extend this play through sustained shared thinking (see page 8). From the age of three to seven years of age children's play moves beyond exploration, and efforts to know and understand become much more than sensory experiences. As children acquire the ability to playfully represent their experiences in a variety of ways and to symbolise the understandings that they have built through exploratory play, they engage in role play and begin to develop narratives for imaginary events. Through this pretend/fantasy play, children extend and develop their understandings of their world.

Role play is an imitation of reality in which children create play "themes" and act them out by participating in various roles. By doing so, they are able to imitate the material world and relationships through symbolic representation. Children select physical objects (e.g. leaves, sticks, balls, baskets, blocks etc), which act as symbols for something else they have experienced directly or indirectly (e.g. babies, pushchairs, swords, boats). For example, children may pretend that a stick is a mobile phone, or that they are Spiderman fighting all the bad guys. Role play is a time of non-literal, symbolic behaviour that merges the child's imagination with the real world[21].

Props to support the use of ICT in role play

Programmable toys provide a particularly useful illustration of 'programming' with the added benefit in terms of gender equality that in many households the adult with the most sophisticated understanding of the complex programmes that are involved are women. In many settings children have created realistic washing machines, microwaves etc. out of junk materials with the support of their teacher and then used these in their classroom role play. We have seen a wide range of props being applied in early years role play contexts, sometimes recycled equipment such as old telephones, visual displays and computer keyboards are incorporated in these 'pretend' technological devices to make them look even more realistic.

Pre-school educators have long recognised that role play, just like any other dramatic improvisation, may be encouraged through the provision of props. Pre-schools therefore include a 'home corner' where scaled-down household furniture and appliances support the children's play at being Mummies, Daddies, as well as babies, pets and many other characters from the home environment. In a similar way ICT education may be supported through the inclusion of ICT props such as 'point of sale' cash registers and bar code scanners, pretend (or working) telephones and computer equipment. Often the props can be made in collaboration with the children developing a play area for a particular topic such as 'At the Vets', 'Going to the Dentist', 'A Travel Agency' or a 'Supermarket' etc. Role projects of this kind are often supported by visits to the appropriate vetinary surgery, travel agents or supermarket and from visits from the professionals working in these contexts visiting the pre-school to talk to the children about their work.

DVD resources are now available from companies such as Early Vision (reference below) who specialise in supporting the development of role play in pre-schools. In their *Travel Agents Role Play Resource* video, customers are shown discussing countries to visit, dates and durations, distance and different forms of transport. The customers book holidays to the Caribbean and Eurodisney, they collect travel tickets and obtain foreign currency. The CD handbook includes role play guidance, writing frames, roles and resources, still photographs, signs, notices, key vocabulary and an EYFS planning sheet. In another example, the 'Going to the Dentist' sequence of their *Ourselves* role play resources, Early Vision provide a video

Software to support role play

In one reception class the *At The Vets* Semerec CD Package was used to support role play in the role play area. Most of the control involves the use of the mouse, but the child also uses the keyboard for typing his or her name and the name of the pet. The child chooses the type of animal, which could be wild or from a farm, and they select the medicine and equipment they need to treat the animal. This activity runs for eight to ten minutes, which is a short enough period of time to keep children focused and interested. The child can also print off an invoice for the treatment, gaining more skills and ICT knowledge as they use the printer.

It was found that the children kept their roles, and were willing to take turns. Each child enjoyed being the vet or veterinary nurse, being the person bringing their pet to the vets and also being the receptionist. The children learnt to put a bandage on, give an injection and give medication to the pet. They enjoyed trying to write their pet's name and also enjoyed copying their own name from their name card. There was a good deal of language being used and all of the children that enjoyed the application, they were all happy and often very excited.

The children were very engaged in the activity, for example, a typical response when clicking on the stethoscope was for a child to share their observation saying: 'The hearts going bom, bom', and when clicking on the key to open the medicine cupboard one child said, 'Mum has a key for her cupboard so we don't touch' ... 'the dog needs to take one tablet'. Then, clicking on the medicine: ' it needs to be taken with his dinner' ... 'yes he likes that, he has licked his lips'.

The teacher reported upon the children's learning associated with their knowledge and understanding of the world, their physical development as they improve their mouse control, their mathematical learning as they used language such as more or less, longer or shorter and also counted out equipment or medication required. The application also encouraged the children to be sympathetic and caring towards animals and to collaborate with each other in the activities.

that shows a reassuring visit by a child to the dentist for an examination. The 'handbook disc' provides a planning support document that can be used to identify other areas of learning that are relevant to the Ourselves topic and also a folder which contains Dentist Photographs, Signs and Notices (to add realism to the play area) and a

Role play

Using metal detectors in a treasure hunt

Although the instructions for the *Discovery World Metal Detectors* suggested they were suitable for children aged eight years and over, a setting in Cambridgeshire was convinced that their children aged between three and four-years-old would be able to operate them safely, and that they would provide a valuable resource for their outdoor play. They even developed a treasure hunt to prove it.

Old metal tins, trays and saucepan lids were buried under a few centimetres of sand in the setting's large outdoor sand pit (measuring approx. 5m x 2.5m). Spades and an old cardboard box (a 'treasure chest') were also provided. At outdoor time the children had a completely free choice of activity and those who came to the sandpit were immediately interested to see the metal detectors that had been provided. The children were shown how to operate the on/off switch and how to walk slowly up and down the sand holding the metal detector close to, but not on, the sand. The children soon learnt to listen for the beep: 'It beeped' ... 'Yeess!' (when it beeped). The treasure hunt soon began, with children calling out; 'We found treasure' and; 'There's no treasure here'. Another child whose machine beeped called 'It's over here. I've found it. I did this'. She immediately demonstrated to the other children how she passed the metal detector over the buried metal making it beep. One child asked: 'How did the metal get here?' and the teacher suggested that perhaps pirates had been to school and buried their treasure: 'I've found metal' ... 'The pirates left it' ... 'There's something shining' ... 'We've found some metal treasure'.

When a child heard a beep and called out 'we've found something' a whole team of diggers descended on the area and started digging collaboratively: a great deal of joy was shared between the children when the 'treasure' was dug up, shown to all, then placed in the 'treasure chest'.

The next day children started making maps in the classroom prior to garden time to help find the treasure. Some had marked 'x' to denote the treasure. Even after the half-term break a child came running up to the teacher at garden time 'Are we having the metal detectors today?' The children continued to be motivated by the activity, they became absorbed in the play, and then went on to extend their experiences to imaginative play in the inside sand trays. It was found that the children quickly gained independent use of the ICT so that after initial instruction the adult intervention required was minimal. The adult then could spend time observing, reinforcing and extending language. It also became a very positive experience for the children to engage with others. The metal detectors were a valuable tool for skill development and collaborative working. The children were able to show each other how to use the equipment. The children's negotiating skills were extended and group decision making was seen. Both boys and girls equally used the metal detectors and did the digging. Also of reported value was the conversation, cooperation, discussion and the thinking that the children used. The range of skill development included hand-eye coordination, concentration and problem solving. Working as a team and the social skill of sharing were noticeably seen, often by children who didn't particularly know each other (from different classes).

Following the treasure hunt activity the teacher planned to develop topic work around the activity involving science (sorting different materials), history (finding old artefacts or treasure perhaps linked to pirates), and geography (map making).

document providing images that illustrate the sort of role play the children might be doing. The resource supports the teachers in their planning and preparation e.g. in identifying the desirability of obtaining some surgical face masks, goggles (or sun glasses), some toothbrushes and a suitable chair for the play area. The latter might be borrowed from a colleague's office for a few weeks. Role play activities such as this provide a context for other integrated topic work, and in this case an obvious extension would involve focusing on teeth (oral) hygiene. The children might be introduced to the 'disclosing tablets' available form most chemists that provide a dye indicator for dental plaque. Their use will help the children to understand the problem and the effectiveness of appropriate brushing. Disposable tongue depressors, children's brushes and even disposable oral inspection mirrors (to be kept in a beaker of antibacterial mouthwash in the role play) are all available for bulk purchase from Internet suppliers (e.g. on ebay).

SEMERC also produce a range of desktop computer software titles to support role play.

Smilansky identified six criteria of dramatic play, the last two of which involve social interaction:

- **Imitative role play:** where the child undertakes a make-believe role, acting it out verbally and physically.

- **Imaginary play with objects:** play behaviours and/or dialogues and/or materials or toys that are not replicas of the object itself, but are substituted for real objects.
- **Verbal make-believe with regard to actions and situations:** where verbal dialogue takes the place of body movements.
- **Persistence in role play:** when the pretend/fantasy play episode is developed and sustained for ten minutes or more.
- **Interaction:** where more than one individual is involved in the same pretend play episode.
- **Verbal communication:** where there is sustained verbal interaction between the players.

Role play, with or without the use of ICT, provides valuable contexts for children to articulate their thinking and to share representations, and it also provides clear opportunities for children and adults to engage in episodes of sustained shared thinking (in clarifying understandings and extending narratives).

There are a great many opportunities for parents and practitioners to embed ICT into young children's pretend play environments. In the modern world children's everyday experiences include:

- Witnessing the use of bar code scanners in shops
- The use of mobile phones
- Digital weighing machines
- Pressing buttons/following directions at a road crossing
- Operating cash machines
- Close circuit television systems
- Using the Internet to buy items.

Within the home a number of machines such as the washing machine, microwave, video and television incorporate computer technology and adults routinely programme a wide range of digital technologies. In fact every role play situation imaginable (indoors and outdoors) could include a number of ICT applications. Traffic lights can be used to support role play activities with outdoor vehicles. Young children can have lots of fun with a metal detector outside, and with using two-way radios for communication. Telephones, cash registers. photocopiers, bar code scanners, and computers, touchscreens can be integrated into imaginary settings such as the computer repair shop, the builders yard, the travel agent, the dinosaur museum, the vets, the post-office and many more…

By supporting fantasy play, early years educators encourage the children to playfully test their understandings of the real world and to separate objects and actions from their meaning in the real world and give them new meanings. Early years educators should also encourage children to communicate and share these creative representations as this provides an important way of developing their powers of expression and abstraction more generally. In fact, towards the end of the pre-school period, some more formal recording and reporting upon their play may provide children with powerful support for their transition to schooling.

Of particular relevance at home

Children frequently develop high levels of confidence and competence with ICT by playing with it informally. It is not unusual for young children to learn to programme digital recordings of favourite TV programmes, or use mobile phones at home through a mixture of observation, trial and error, and support from a 'knowledgeable other'.

Role play

As they begin to take an interest, parents can share with children the experience of talking to family and friends on a mobile telephone, and even through email. Skype now provide a powerful, reliable (and free) video telephone service over the Internet and we have seen this used effectively with young children under close adult supervision.

A project developed in one school illustrated the possibilities for extending children's awareness of ICT through engagement with family travels. In one school the teacher's parents went on a cruise. The children followed the ship's progress through the P&O web site, had email updates from their teacher's parents sent from the ship on a regular basis, and the children created a mock up of a ship's bridge for role play in their classroom.

■ TTS products, including international sales: (http://www.tts-group.co.uk).

[20] Vygotsky, L. (19) *Mind in Society: The Development of Higher Psychological Processes.* Harvard University Press, Cambridge Mass: 4.

[21] Smilansky, S. (196) *The Effects of Sociodramatic Play on Disadvantaged Preschool Children.* John Wiley and Sons: New York.

Resources

■ At the Vets
At the Toy Shop
At the Garden Centre
At the Post Office
At the Vets
At the Doctors
At the Café
All available from Semerc (http://www.semerc.com/).

■ Travel Agents Play Pack
Airport role play
The Café
The Doctors
Estate Agents
Ourselves
The Garage
The Police
The Post Office
The Train Station
The Travel Agents
from Early Vision (http://www.earlyvision.co.uk/).

■ Traffic lights, measuring 72cm, are currently available for £19.99 excluding batteries from Early Years Resources (http://www.earlyyearsresources.co.uk).

■ *Metal Detectors* are currently available as children's toys from Argos (http://www.argos.co.uk).

■ Skype allows Internet users to make free video calls (http://www.skype.com).

■ 2Simple products:
USA (http://www.2simpleusa.com)
Australia (http://www.2simple.com.au)
Singapore (http://www.verticalmiles.com).

Using ICT in the home environment

ICT capability

A growing consensus has developed in recent years that it is the development of ICT capability, rather than ICT skills, that should be the central focus of ICT in education in the early years and beyond. ICT skills are routines, techniques and processes such as knowing how to use the mouse, clicking on the correct icon to save work, learning how to view a digital image on the screen. ICT capability is considered the ability to utilise ICT independently, appropriately and creatively and to understand ICT in its social context. The notion of ICT capability therefore implies an ability to act in future situations and involves learning about its potential for use. We know that confidence gained from playing with ICT will support the development of ICT capability in more formal contexts as the child gets older. Yet children's ability to develop ICT capability via playful activity has often ignored or suppressed in school classrooms rather than supported and respected[22]. One of the most useful summaries of ICT capability[23] identifies five key components:

- **Routines** – how to use a graphics tablet or a touchscreen can be learned. It is impossible to achieve a high level of ICT capability without this content knowledge and most young children master these skills very quickly. Such skills are however of no value at all unless the child has a purpose in mind.
- **Techniques** – inserting a photo into a document. The majority of interfaces and navigation techniques for different applications are similar, which aids transfer of learning.
- **Processes** – where techniques are combined e.g. to produce a greetings card or a poster
- **Key concepts** – including the basic terminology/shared vocabulary that enables children to communicate effectively and understand what is required of them.
- **Higher order skills and knowledge** – where children clearly exhibit an understanding of what they are

doing. They select appropriate equipment, routines, techniques and processes to obtain a desired outcome. This is developed through exploratory play with ICT where children have the opportunity to reflect on past experiences. Higher order skills are demonstrated when young children:

- Decide when it is appropriate to use a particular ICT for a specific purpose
- Plan what routines, techniques and processes are to be used
- Work independently to solve problems
- Evaluate their use of ICT and the outcome of an activity
- Explain and justify their choices and approaches
- Reflect on their learning and how things could be approached differently next time.

The first three of these routines, techniques and processes can be learned indirectly, through trial-and-error, via interaction with an adult or through a combination of all of these. The successful development of the final two key components require that adults support children's learning with technology by engaging in episodes of sustained shared thinking.

There are additional evidence-based strategies that might usefully complement the use of SST with young children to support their emergent literacy development. Emergent literacy can be understood as the time prior to conventional reading and writing. It encompasses the range of knowledge, skills, experiences and attitudes which children need to be exposed to and develop as pre-cursors to conventional literacy[24]. As an example, young children tend to understand functions of print (that print carries meaning) before later starting to recognise letters and words.

One well-tested strategy is print referencing[25] which is a technique shown to increase:

often been found to have highly involved parents who play with their children at the keyboard, entering into dialogue and offer encouragement as well as practical assistance with the programme.

Enriched language environments

Studies[20] have shown that middle-class parents speak, on average, 300 words per hour to their children, and that the vocabulary gap between children at age three correlates strongly with their subsequent language performance in school. We know that children more advanced in their reading capabilities are usually brought up in an environment that has exposed them to a significantly larger vocabulary. The average one-year-old has about five words in their vocabulary on average, although some may have none and others as many as 30. At age two, an average child's vocabulary is more than 150 words (with a range of between 10 and 450 words). Children have a vocabulary of about 14,000 words at six years of age and the average adult (at age 40) has a working vocabulary of about 40,000 words. In order to achieve this it is clear that children must be learning at least a few new words every day.

Parents and practitioners in partnership

As suggested earlier, parenting practices and learning opportunities provided in the home are associated with better educational outcomes. This partly explains the links that have been identified between socio-economic status and educational outcomes. Middle-class parents tend to provide their children with more learning opportunities. However, the research indicates that where otherwise disadvantaged parents provide a rich learning environment for their children, those children go on to succeed in education in their later life. When it comes to the home learning environment **it is what you do**, rather than **who you are** that really matters! Parental involvement in the form of 'at-home good parenting' has a significant positive effect on children's achievement and adjustment even after all other factors shaping attainment have been taken out of the equation. In the primary age range the impact caused by different levels of parental involvement is much bigger than differences associated with variations in the quality of schools. The scale of the impact is evident across all social classes and all ethnic groups[31].

A number of researchers studying older children have also stressed the importance of parental involvement in children's computer use at home[21]. One of the most important findings has been that the level of children's use of computers in school is directly influenced by their out of school experiences.

In the early years, ICT has a major contribution to make in enhancing the home learning environment. Our current research suggests that the best practice occurs where adults (or more capable peers) recognise play as an educationally profitable and valuable experience in itself. They apply ICTs to interact playfully with children adopting a style of play that always follows the child's lead, but also enhances and extends the dialogue to achieve sustained shared thinking (for more on sustained shared thinking see page 8). In the following pages we identify a range of software that may be used to support this practice. Increasingly, software will also become available that has been designed specifically to serve these ends (some of the most exciting work in this area may be seen at: http:www.madeinme.co.uk and http://www.futurelab.org.uk).

Research suggests that communication between the home and school leads to better understanding and more positive attitudes for teachers and parents about each other's roles. Many studies have shown that children achieve more academically when parents, teachers and children all collaborate towards the same goals. Parent involvement is, therefore, a component of effective schools and pre-schools which merits special consideration. Communication between professional educators and parents is especially important in the early years and a more articulated set of aims between the home and early years setting can lead to better outcomes for children. In one pre-school setting, parental involvement is encouraged through many aspects of children's learning. The staff involve parents through:

- The use of digital, still and video images in the entrance lobby, recording trips, a typical day's activities, curriculum presentations, and any special events
- The use of digital pictures in children's records
- Email communication between the centre staff and parents
- Asking parents to try out new software
- The use of closed circuit television to enable parents to watch children at play and learning
- The loan of cassette recorders and other ICT equipment to take home
- Making CD-Roms of children singing
- The development of the nursery website.

The specific contribution that can be made by pre-schools

The EPPE research has emphasised the importance of the home learning environment (HLE) but it has also demonstrated the value of pre-school provision and also the importance of quality in pre-school education. This project applied standardised observation scales that included ratings of adult-child interaction in measuring quality. Children with a poor early HLE were found to benefit from attending a medium quality pre-school, but they were found to gain significantly more from pre-schools identified as 'high quality'. EPPE found that some families offer a rich HLE, and some pre-schools offer excellent pre-school learning experiences. In either case, the child can be 'protected' from an otherwise disadvantaged family background and go on to succeed in education. The issue of quality was found to be critical in both the home and the pre-school learning environments with children who experienced high quality learning at home and at pre-school benefiting the most.

The proliferation of ICT within the home has to some extent been paralleled with developments within pre-schools. Whilst there has been some evidence from early years research that computer-based, formal 'drill and practice' instruction can show short-term gains, it has also been found that this approach to learning can impact negatively on both young

children's emotional well-being and their dispositions to learning. The approach has therefore been considered inappropriate for use in the early years and beyond. The most appropriate approach of using ICT to support early learning has been an emergent one, where the emphasis has been upon the children seeing ICT being used in meaningful contexts and for real purposes. In terms of successfully supporting emergent ICT in the pre-school sector the Developmentally Appropriate Technology in Early Childhood (DATEC) research found that the best applications were those that:

- Were demonstrably educational
- Encouraged collaboration
- Supported the integration of ICT across both the curriculum and across the pedagogy of the pre-school
- Supported play
- Left the child in control of the interaction
- Were transparent, intuitive and understandable from the child's perspective
- Avoided violence or stereotyping
- Supported the development of children's awareness of health and safety issues
- Supported the involvement of parents.

Perhaps the most contentious of these recommended features is the first bullet point above – and for this reason we have been at pains to be clear in the following pages in what way we consider the ICTs suggested offer educational value. In the past some people have suggested that children should have access to computers simply to learn about 'mouse' and 'keyboard' skills. One of the problems with that idea is that the QWERTY keyboard layout was originally developed to stop the mechanical type from jamming together when people typed too fast on mechanical typewriters. It was designed to slow the typist down by separating out all the most commonly used keys. Maybe we could possibly come up with something better sometime soon. The best technologies are ones that require little or no instruction to operate. Their operation is intuitive. Touch screens are already the preferred interface for all kinds of mobile technology and voice recognition systems are improving all the time.

Desktop computers are already old technology ... and it would be difficult to argue that we should be teaching children about them as they will be significant in their future lives. We shouldn't be basing our educational provisions on learning how to use them – most four-year-olds will probably have forgotten they ever existed before they leave school and go out to work. Computers are tools like blackboards and easels, like typewriters and telephones, there are even forms of computer that are already entirely redundant. There would be little point in teaching children about optical card readers or computer tape drives although they both revolutionised industries and ways of working in their time.

Since Barbara Tizard and Martin Hughes'[32] research studies in the 1980s we have been aware that, whilst conversational exchanges in the home may at times be relatively rich and encourage active participation on the part of the children, exchanges in the nursery school between adults and children are often relatively impoverished, with teachers posing a series of closed questions, rather than fostering open-ended conversations. A number of studies have also found that preschool educators are rarely present when children are using desktop computers. None of this is particularly surprising when you consider the typical adult to child ratios applied in pre-schools. While research suggests that qualified teachers are more likely to be present at the computer, even then adult support is very rarely extended beyond a minute or two at a time. In the majority of cases, adult support is limited to a brief intervention when the children experience problems or require supervision. It seems that most children are left to develop their computing skills independently, with preschool educators questioning, instructing and managing only when necessary. One important consequence of encouraging pre-schools to work with parents to support children with computers in the home may therefore be to raise awareness of the issues and to improve provisions in the pre-schools as well. Many of the ICT applications that we identify throughout the book provide valuable structured activities that pre-school teachers can introduce to adult helpers, support staff, or peer tutors within the pre-school setting, as well as promoting their use in the home.

As suggested earlier, the pre-school sector has a long history of working with parents in supporting children's emergent literacy. Work in this area has always emphasised the importance of the processes of interaction involved with parents and children engaged together in a shared process of meaning making. ICT parental partnership initiatives may be considered a logical extension of these established 'shared reading' practices.

The curriculum contexts of England, Wales, Scotland and Northern Ireland

There is currently different curriculum guidance for early years in England, Wales, Scotland and Northern Ireland. Each has a slightly different approach to ICT in the early years but all place an emphasis on its use to develop ICT capability.

Research evidence has shown that the efforts of parents and preschools can make a considerable difference to children's future educational achievements regardless of their socio-economic background. Current national policy initiatives that aim to close the gap in educational achievement for children from disadvantaged backgrounds are ambitious but they should therefore be recognised as credible. Research suggests that there may now be a real possibility of creating a level playing field for future educational achievement at age five for all but the most disabled children. The Children's Plan in England is clear in its recognition that this can only be achieved in partnership with parents. One of the ways in which this commitment has manifested itself has been in the Government's £300m Home Access project which provides computers and Internet access to families to enhance learning at home. It is important that this should now be extended to provide for the pre-school period.

ICTs in early childhood have the potential to make a major contribution to the more general policy initiatives associated with achieving higher educational standards, social justice and equality of opportunity. We hope that this book will make a modest contribution towards realising this potential.

Vicarious learning in early childhood

Vicarious learning is also known as observational learning or modelling; it describes learning that occurs when individuals observe, retain and are able to replicate the actions of others. Children learn a great deal from observing adults and other children's use of ICT, and in the early years adult modelling behaviour is particularly powerful. One of the most significant sources for children to learn new routines, techniques and processes is in observing their use by their early years educators. 2Simple have produced some extremely valuable tools for this purpose in their *Infant Video Toolkit 2*. The toolkit includes *2Paint, 2Publish, 2Count, 2Graph, 2Go, 2Graph and 2Question*. Each program provides open-ended tools that may be applied to support collaborative small or large group activities and dialogues. *2Count and 2Graph* provide exceptionally intuitive tools for creating a variety of pictograms, histograms and pie charts, and *2Question* provides a branching database for constructing and recording a wide range of sorting activities including the use of classifications for animals, plants and materials.

The package provides an introduction, overview with a description and curriculum links for each of the program available, as well as 75 example video lessons which provide instructions on how to use the tools and some ideas for application.

Each programme uses the same control interface so that the children can quickly learn to print, create a new page or exit for themselves.

Three other 2Simple products worth a particular mention as tools that may be used particularly effectively applied by the teacher long before the children begin using them on their own are the 2Simple Music Toolkit, 2Create a story, 2Animate and 2DIY.

A very successful ICT project that has been set up in a few pre-school and school settings has employed the use of webcams in bird boxes. This allows children to discuss and consider the use of ICT for a purpose.

Of particular relevance at home

At home, just as in the pre-school setting, a great deal can be done to provide children with positive models for applying a range of ICTs.

Many children are already gaining a rich online experience from sharing online shopping expeditions with their parents.

Children can also contribute in preparing materials to be sent to distant relatives by email (or Skype). In this way children's paintings and drawings may be shared, and even recordings of their voice messages may be sent by email (if you haven't already, plug in a microphone and try out the voice recorder included in the Microsoft Accessories folder).

Resources

▨ Infant Video Toolkit 2 and the other programs mentioned in this chapter are available from http://www.2simpleshop.com/
A number of these programs are available for home use from the 2simple home shop.
2Simple products are also available in:
USA: http://www.2simpleusa.com
Australia: www.2simple.com.au
Singapore: www.verticalmiles.com

▨ Information on capturing and streaming images from birdboxes can be found at http://birdbox.segfl.org.uk/

▨ Skype allows Internet users to make free video calls (http://www.skype.com).

Handy hints and tips

Don't just consider the suitability of software tools from the perspective of children's use on their own. The children will benefit from seeing you use many other software tools developed for adult use, or for use by older children.

[22] Facer K, Furlong J, Furlong R et al (2003). ScreenPlay: Children and computing in the home. Routledge: London

[23] Kennewell S, Parkinson J, Tanner H (2000) Developing the ICT capable school. Routledge: London

[24] Clay, M.M. (2000). Concepts about print: What have children learned about the way we print language? Portsmouth, NH: Heinemann.

[25] Zucker, T. A., Justice, L. M., & Piasta, S. B. (2009). Pre-kindergarten teachers' verbal references to print during classroom-based large-group shared reading. Journal of Language, Speech, and Hearing Services in the Schools, 40, 376–392.

[26] Zucker, T. A., Justice, L. M., & Piasta, S. B. (2009). Pre-kindergarten teachers' verbal references to print during classroom-based large-group shared reading. Journal of Language, Speech, and Hearing Services in the Schools, 40, 376–392.

[27] Zucker, T., Ward, A., & Justice, L. M. (2009). Print- referencing during read-alouds: Examining a technique for increasing emergent readers' print knowledge. Reading Teacher.

[28] Sylva, K., Melhuish, E., Siraj-Blatchford, I. et al. (2008) The Effective Pre-School and Primary Education (EPPSE 3-11) project: final report. London: DCSF.

[29] Fish, M. A., Li, X., McCarrick, K.,Butler, S. T., Stanton, B. Brumitt, G. A. Bhavnagri N. B., Holtrop T. Partridge, T. (2008) Early Childhood Computer Experience and Cognitive Development Among Urban Low-Income Preschoolers. Journal of Educational Computing Research 38(1) 97-113.

[30] Hart, B. and Risley, T.R. (1995) Meaningful Differences in the Everyday Experience of Young American Children. Brookes Publishing. New York.

[31] Desforges,C. and Abouchaar, A. (2003) The Impact of Parental Involvement, Parental Support and Family Education on Pupil Achievement and Adjustment: A Literature Review. DfES Research Report 433.

[32] Tizard, B. & Hughes, M. (1984) Young Children learning, Fontana.

Adventure and simulation games

Many parents and practitioners will consider much of the adventure and simulation games genres to be far too demanding for young children, however both have a great deal of potential to make a significant contribution to developing young children's thinking. They can provide a playful arena to develop children's confidence as learners and provide opportunities for them to work collaboratively and creatively as problem solvers.

To understand which programmes are most appropriate for use with young children, we need to consider carefully how adventure games and simulations function, and therefore how they might best be used to support the development of thinking and learning.

Adventure games

Adventure games focus on puzzle solving within a narrative framework. The way we 'see' a problem in our mind influences how we attempt to solve it and therefore our chances of being successful in doing so. Adventure games support children's emergent skills as thinkers by allowing them a contextualised opportunity to identify what is useful and what is not in solving a puzzle. The best examples of these demand some engagement in logical thought and so provide sufficient cognitive challenge for young children to engage in episodes of sustained shared thinking with an older child or adult. They provide opportunities for what is sometimes referred to as 'the development of thinking skills', but may simply be considered 'hard fun'!

How do they do this? There is usually a strong narrative (a good story). Many adventure games for children are an extension of a narrative with which they may already be familiar e.g. Bob the Builder or Peppa Pig. There basically needs to be a reason for a child to want to invest time engaging with a complex problem – just as there is in

the real world. Engaging these real world emotions is an essential element of establishing motivation and purpose.

It should be noted that adventure games are very different from action (arcade) games which feature high-speed, physical drama and often make high demands of players in terms of physical interaction, reflexes and coordination skills while requiring low levels of cognitive interaction with others. Many of these games are labelled as adventure games and are marketed as 'edutainment'. In reality however, many are simply hybrids of an arcade game and some drill and practice software. The use of these with young children in educational settings is inappropriate.

To summarise, the educational potential of adventure games, is widely considered to provide:

- An environment in which high levels of motivation exist to encourage playful problem solving
- An opportunity to clearly represent a problem and to identify the types of information relevant to its solution
- An environment in which it is possible to collect and organise the relevant information
- To facilitate the development of a strategic approach
- To support the development of reasoning by encouraging the development and testing of hypothesis using a range of approaches.

What do we need to avoid in adventure games?

- Action-type games which do not provide the opportunity for problem solving, creativity and collaboration
- Games which promote gender bias
- Games which contain excessive violence.

There are a number of examples of appropriate desk or laptop computer adventure games for use with young children, these include *Bob's Castle Adventure, Peppa Pig Puddles of Fun* and *Dora Explorer*. Piglet's Big Game is also an adventure game for the Playstation and the Land Me series, *Tillies Time Shop* and *Monsters Socks* apps also have a lot of potential on the iPad. Very able or older children have also benefited from Carmen Sandiego Junior Detective, Dieago's Safari Adventure, Crystal Forest's *The Logical Journey of the Zoombinis* and Rebelmind Studios Great Journey.

Bob's Castle Adventure

This adventure game includes a number of games with different themes, maze games, castle walls games, moat games and dungeon games. Each of these can be played at three levels of difficulty: easy, medium or hard. This ensures that there is a sufficient level of cognitive challenge to allow for meaningful interaction between the child or children and adults when playing this adventure game.

Adults should consider the value of taking control, or at least a turn with the mouse when using this program, as this can prove valuable in developing and extending dialogue and sustained shared thinking. When the child has control of the mouse there will be less 'thinking out loud'.

During the dungeon game, Spotting Spiders, Bob is in the dungeons searching for treasure. He wonders if anything is behind the door ... there is, but it is covered with spiders! Bob needs to chase the spiders away with his torchlight by moving the light over them with the mouse. If the torch is not on the spider for long enough it will return. Players need to develop a strategy to clear all the spiders from the door. This provides opportunity for dialogue with purpose in an entertaining and playful context.

Simulations

Computer simulations are used to represent real or imaginary situations (often a hybrid of both). They allow children to attempt and study things which would be impossible or very difficult in the real world. They are particularly valuable where the activity would be too fast or slow, dangerous or expensive to undertake. In practice, early childhood simulations may be as simple as a screen version of a potato 'face maker' or 'dress teddy' program, or as sophisticated as a duck 'flight simulator' or 'Soup Toys' (see next page). Simulations are also valuable where they allow young children to identify patterns and relationships and to make and explore predictions. They allow children to playfully engage in a process of trial and

error where the feedback on the decisions made are clear and easy to interpret.

They allow children to form hypothesis, via a process of trial and error in a range of simplified contexts. Applying the concepts and skills developed in one to another.

Simulations are highly valued by professional adult scientists for precisely the same reasons. They provide a simplified model of complex real world problems. This makes the problem and the potential solution easier to 'see', whilst remaining contextualised enough to be reasonably realistic.

Souptoys.com provides a free to download collection of 'virtual' toys, that mostly react "realistically" on your desktop. If you want a toy, you just drag it out of the Toybox and onto your desktop. If you have the resources many of the simulated activities on screen can also be played off screen. When you first load the program a 'wooden' toybox appears. Simple controls allow you

Adventure and simulation games

Exploring The Duck Builder software together

Adult is sitting alone exploring The Duck Builder software.
Child sits down next to them.
Child: Can I try it?
Adult: Have you seen this program before?
Child: No – is it a bird?
Adult: Yes that is right, its a duck. A duck is a type of bird.
Child: Can we do that?
Child points to the fly button.
Adult: OK.
Adult presses the fly button. The duck takes off from the runway and crashes to the ground.
Child: (*Laughs*) He is dead now haha. Again?
Adult: So do you think that the same thing will happen again?
Child: (*nods and models the bird's trajectory to the ground with his hand*).
Adult: Let us see shall we.......
Adult presses the fly button. The duck takes off from the runway and crashes to the ground.
Child: I want to make him go up now.
Adult: Ok so what shall we do?
Child: Make this big (pointing to the beak).
Adult: So do you think that having a big beak will make the duck fly up?
Child: (shrugs shoulders) I don't know?
Adult: Shall we try it out and see what happens with a big beak?
Child: Yes like that, very big like that. No smaller, yes like that.
Adult: Is there any thing else you would like to try?
Child: No, fly now.
Adult presses the fly button. The duck takes off from the runway and crashes to the ground.

Child: (Laughs) Look, it does the same!
Adult: what do you mean?
Child: With a big ...
Adult: Beak.
Child: Yes it goes down with a big ....
Adult: Beak.
Child: I want it to fly.
Adult: Ok, shall we try again?
Child: (Nods) What shall we try next?
Child: Small beak.
Adult: Ok, this small?
Child: (Nods).
Adult: Shall we make him flap like this (fast), or like this (slow)?
Child: Like this (flaps his arms vigorously and quickly).
Adult: Ok.
Child : Yes like that, now fly!
Adult presses the fly button. The duck takes off from the runway and flies up to outer space where it is met by an alien ship.
Child: (laughter) Ha ha that was funny. (Pause) Can we make it crash again?
Adult: (laughter) Ok what do you think we should do?
Child: Try this (points to the legs).
Adult: Like this (big) or this (smaller)?
Child: Big legs and big beak and like this (flaps arms slowly).
Adult: Ok, so what do you think will happen this time?
Child: Crash!
Adult: Why?
Child: Like this (flaps arms slowly) is a crash (laughter).
Adult presses the fly button. The duck takes off from the runway and crashes to the ground. Child gets up from chair and moves away from the computer.
Child: Yes it did it. That was funny!

---

to cover your desktop with a temporary background and then drag and drop a selection of toys out of the box. These include building blocks, balls, a snowball firing cannon, too many options to list here. Playing with SoupToys may be entirely exploratory and open-ended, or more usefully if we want to encourage sustained shared thinking, the adult can suggest a particular challenge or problem to be solved. One example might be to begin the by making a tower together out of bricks. You can make joint decisions on what coloured blocks, rectangles and triangles will be placed each time, and take turns in using the mouse to drag and adjust the bricks into position. If at any point you can 'Rewind' your choice or press a button to 'Clear' the screen . When the tower is built you can scroll down on through the Toy sets and choose Christmas Toys. Then drag out the Snowball Cannon and a drum.

The problem that can then be solved is for you to thrown snowballs over the top of the tower to hit and sound on the drum on the other side without disturbing the tower (In season you might like to replace the tower with a decorated Christmas tree). You may also wish to put some snowmen around the tower to see what happens when they get hit by a snowball...Souptoys has Tutorial and Help pages and a vast selection of toys and resources to draw upon in developing your own problems to solve.

The point of undertaking a simulation is not to get a predetermined 'right' answer but to experiment with changing a range of variables and to investigate the relationship between cause and effect. Simulations help children to make predictions, 'If I change this I think this might happen' and to move from what to why questions,

'If I change this I think this will happen because ...' When using simulations with young children practitioners and parents should encourage children to explore a range of outcomes and make predictions and develop ideas about the relationships between changes in variables and different outcomes. For the youngest children especially, the adult shouldn't worry too much about getting the 'right' answers, the child will enjoy (and benefit from) simply exploring the various outcomes produced.

The Duck Builder simulation game, available to download free from http://www.cgpbooks.co.uk/duckBuilder, offers the opportunity for adults and children to work in precisely this way. The wing length, leg length, beak length, body size and flap speed of a duck can all be changed within set parameters. There are three possible outcomes: (i) the duck can fly straight ahead (ii) the duck can fly into space (and be met by an alien space ship) (iii) the duck can crash to the ground.

Our trials have shown us that the adult-child interaction is improved when playing this game if the adult has control of the mouse but the child remains in control of the decisions regarding what variables should be changed. The child may be given full control over the degree to which the variables are changed by using the keyboard arrow keys, but these are only effective when the adult has selected the appropriate slider using the mouse. The adults selection of the particular slider therefore provides them with sufficient influence over the action to retain their involvement in a dialogue. The adult can develop the child (or even a small group of children's) thinking during the interaction by supporting and developing their ideas and by encouraging both the making of predictions and the consideration of cause and effect.

'The Land of Me'

The Land of Me software series has been developed specifically to maximise the potential for sustained shared thinking by parents and children engaged in screen playing together. Six titles are available for PC and Mac and three of these are also available as Apps for the iPad2. There are also 'samples' of the software available for free download for each platform. *The Land of Me* brings children through a series of adventures involving the three main characters: Eric, Willow and Buddy, a racoon, a bird, and a large bear. Children built a bond with the characters and look forward each time they go to another part of Land of Me where they learn about: Shape, Size and Colour, The World Outside, Making Things, Rhythm and Dance, Songs and Rhymes, and Story Time. Each site is hosted by a different character/creature: a snow monkey, a vulture, a bear and so on.

Handy hints and tips

Promote collaboration, communication and discussion when using adventure games and simulations to support interactions with children. Use open-ended questioning (see transcript on the opposite page). Consider opportunities for children to record their thinking about their electronic experiences with adventure games and simulations as drawings. Where appropriate these may be used as prompts for further discussion or exploration.

Story Time (for example) is available for free download from the App Store for the iPad2 (IPAD2 only). In Story Time Granny Olive (a turtle) tells tales about wolves, bravery and things that go bump in the night! The program allows the child to create their own stories by choosing the hero, the theme and how it ends. You can change the words to instantly alter the storyline as it plays out in front of you and the on-screen hints offer ideas for discussion and things to do. Copy the symbols onto cards and an even wider range of stories can be planned and played out in role off screen.

The Land of Me programs provide an iconic vocabulary of images for the children to play with in their imagination. The products of the children's creations are also presented in text that can be changed by the adult at the request of the child. As these words are edited, animations are directly changed on the screen to provide the adult with a means of demonstrating the power and value of textual language, and to encourage the child's motivation to develop these skills, and their emergent literacy in the future. When the adult clicks on a scissors symbol they can also access a range of activities to do away from the screen at home. There are things to make, songs and lyrics to download, and videos showing the real animals that are included in the animations.

Of particular relevance at home

Avoid violent or edutainment-type arcade games which provide very limited opportunities for collaboration, communication and creative approaches to problem solving. Select adventure games which contain games or problems to be solved which allow for meaningful interaction between children and other family members.

Consider how the strategies that you can draw on to support sustained shared thinking (see page 8) can be used to develop and extend the verbal interaction.

When using simulations or adventure games, rather than focusing on achieving the 'right answer', develop episodes of Sustained Shared Thinking with the child (which may include lots of playful reciprocal activity and laughter).

Imaging movies and graphics

Image, movie and graphics hardware and software can be used in a wide variety of ways to support learning in the early years. They can be used to facilitate children's investigation of their environment, providing a means of viewing phenomenon otherwise inaccessible, e.g. using a digital microsope or viewing a wildlife area at night. They also allow children to observe specific events or features closely with the support of a practitioner who can support them to explore and reflect on ideas which emerge from the observations.

Digital cameras

Digital cameras record images electronically as digital files, which can be downloaded onto a computer for viewing, manipulating and printing. Digital cameras selected for use with young children should be robust and straightforward to use and understand. Like all early childhood hardware and software it should be selected according to its functional transparency. In particular, it should be apparent how the image is transferred from the camera to the computer. Children should be able to remove the memory card from the camera and place in the computer, or connect the camera to the interface 'shoe' and then double-click on the thumbnail image to open the digital image on the screen. If a camera with a USB cable is to be used then it is worth spending a little time creating the appropriate desktop shortcut icons to simplify the process. The advantage of this is that images are available immediately and the child is able to follow the stages of the process involved. The ability to record, access and manipulate images immediately means that they can be used in a variety of ways in early years settings:

- To document learning and communicate this with parents where the focus is the process of learning in addition, to or rather than, a product.

- To reflect on specific learning episodes with children and to use the images as a prompt to engage them in future planning.
- To develop relationships with children and families by encouraging children to share their own favourite people, places and activities from outside the setting.
- To support role play e.g. by taking digital photos of sick animals and using the negative effect in a photo editor to us this in an animal hospital role play.
- To use digital images of a familiar event (e.g. nativity play, school day) to discuss sequencing events and to develop the concept of narrative.

While the *Microsoft Paint* (Windows Accessories folder) menu systems is generally unsuitable for use by young children in their own, the software provides a very quick and simple means of re-sizing, annotating and reformatting (e.g. for Jpeg conversion) the children's digital images. Also, where this is carried out in children's presence it provides yet another valuable context for indirect learning.

Producing moving images

Many digital cameras are now able to capture movie clips as well as still images. Short video clips can be easily recorded using a child-friendly camera and uploaded via a USB connection or using a mobile phone and uploaded via Bluetooth or email. There is also a wide range of editing software available (e.g. iMovie, Windows MovieMaker).

There are many aspects of moving image production which might usefully be explored in early years settings. These include:

- Event filming: filming events and activities from daily life
- Filming for a purpose e.g. to inform younger siblings or about 'what we do at nursery'

- Creating a record of the process and product of a creative process, such as a poem, painting or musical composition
- Creating digital animations (see Marsh, 2008).

These experiences allow young children to develop:

- Technical skills (e.g. controlling the mouse, using the editing software)
- Visual skills (e.g. framing shots)

Using the digital camera

The children's evaluations of using digital cameras were self-explanatory, all wanted more turns, and could not stop showing classroom visitors, parents and peers their photographs.

Child E said: 'Hey look at this, it's a digital camera you can take it to the computer and see your picture on the screen'.

The children used the camera and shared their enjoyment visibly and in their work. Excited sounds were heard as it was their turn, some used it easily, others were fast and furious and needed support to understand how to see the image. The co-ordination and concentration required by some to photograph was immense. But no child was fazed or anxious once using it – quite the reverse; we had to have a tick list to monitor 'goes' on the camera! The contrast with offers of goes with the other camera, which wasn't digital, was striking, I asked several children why they wanted more time on the digital version, and their response was clear:

Child M said: 'This is a real camera and you get real pictures.' I showed her that we had taken many real photos with the other camera, she responded by saying that you did not know what it looked like until the prints came back from the chemist. After we had used the camera, I asked the children what they thought of digital cameras. Should we use one again?

Child H said: 'YES. It was wicked, you can see the whole school through the window on the camera.'

Child F said: 'You don't have to buy films, you need a disk and we have those in school.'

When asked if they thought we should buy one for our class, one child said that he thought we needed one each as 'we might want to have one in our tray so we could take pictures of all we do, every day'!

- An understanding of narrative (e.g. creating stories),
- The concept of multimodality (e.g. by considering the addition of sound)
- An awareness of audience (e.g. by considering if peers would be interested and why)
- Critical skills (e.g. identifying features which were successful or which needed changing).

Recording and discussing a role play

In a Year 1 classroom in Wales children had been role playing a hospital as part of their daily provision for a few weeks. The children were invited to develop a scene for filming in which someone who was unwell went to see the doctor. The children were keen to dress up as medical personnel and entered into the role play with much enthusiasm. They planned and rehearsed the planned scenario in English and Welsh, using some of the language patterns and Welsh vocabulary they had been learning at school.

Imaging movies and graphics

One child was designated as the camera person, while the others acted out the practiced scene. There were clearly some interesting tensions here between the children's desire to learn to use the digital blue cameras autonomously and engage (and improvise) in the hospital role play activity, and the teacher's planned outcomes for the session, which was the development of predetermined language patterns and Welsh vocabulary.

The children sat with the teacher to review their performance showing an interest in developing the target language for a specific purpose, to improve their story.

The teacher commented on how useful she found the opportunity to discuss this activity with the children and to develop an understanding of their perspectives on the activity. She felt that this might be useful in informing future planning.

This experience allowed the children to use video to develop their understanding of narrative, an awareness of audience and, for some, increased the motivation to develop vocabulary in a target second language.

Paint programmes

A number of paint programmes suitable for use in early years settings are available with broadly similar features (*RM Colour Magic 3, 2Paint a Picture, Textease, CT Paint, 2Simple Infant Video Toolkit – 2Paint*). *Tux Paint* is an open

Using a webcam without an Internet connection

Webcams typically provide excellent value for money. They provide inexpensive video cameras for the children to use for a variety of purposes. They usually come with a long USB lead (and you can get USB extension leads if it isn't long enough), video management software is also typically provided along with the facility to take stills as well as movies. The control interface on many webcams is as simple as (and very similar to) that of a cassette recorder i.e. you are given play and record buttons, and a rewind facility.

Filming for a purpose

In one nursery the teacher had worked with the children to make their own 'Teach Me' videos. Each child was encouraged to think of some special technique, skill, or knowledge they had that they could teach to the other children. Some chose things as simple as cutting a piece of coloured paper into a spiral to make a spinning mobile and another recited a poem from memory. Each was recorded as short videos with the webcam. The webcam software presented each of the videos as a table of thumbprint opening frames which the children could browse through and double click to play their choice. This provided a popular choice of activity that may have been contributing significantly to the children's awareness of learning and learning to learn.

Digital microscopes

Digital microscopes allow access to the microscopic world and offer the opportunity to view the results electronically and to digitally document these. The images produced can be saved or manipulated by using the software which comes with the microscope. Some microscopes may also be used in hand-held mode or in the fixed mode. Young children enjoy using these to investigate parts of the body, different fabrics, flowers and leaves, seeds and especially insects at close magnification.

source (free to download version (see **Resources** page 32). Young children are able to develop confidence and competence with this type of simple graphical user-interface easily. Through using this type of software young children learn to recognise icons, and to associate them with specific functions. They are generally confident to experiment and learn how to use the software by watching others, through trial and error and by engaging in discussion with a practitioner or more capable peer whilst engaged on a specific task.

If you are using a typical desktop computer setup with a mouse, probably the least useful thing that you could do with paint software in the earl with. However skilled they were it is extremely unlikely that any real life graphic designer or artist would use a computer mouse for this purpose. Pencils are far superior when it comes to drawing a picture. But, what the computer paint software can do admirably (and would also be used by professionals to do), is 'fill' colours, duplicate images, and apply clip art 'stamps'. To make the most of a paint programme you should therefore invest in a flatbed scanner as well. Then the children can draw their pictures using the traditional methods, and then scan them in order to 'finish' them. There are also numerous transferrable techniques that they will learn along the way, such as the need to ensure that all spaces are 'filled' using the software 'paintpot' and there is no gap in the line for the virtual paint to spill out.

As suggested above, paint programmes can be used to manipulate digital photographs. They can also be used to explore the vocabulary and concepts relating to shape, colour, pattern (repeating patterns) and symmetry.

Sharing observations and assessment with parents: e-portfolios

ICT has widely been considered valuable in supporting children's learning and for reporting to parents. The best practices use the technology on a daily basis to provide documentation of learning and formative assessment. Some settings have developed their practice to involve the parents themselves in these processes of documentation.

In Northamptonshire some early success was reported on the use of Personal Digital Assistants (PDAs or palm-held technology).

They were found easy to use by children and by the adults, who used them to add materials to e-portfolios. They were placed in activity areas as part of the continuous provision for children to use. Some settings have also been piloting the use of email to develop a dialogue between parents, children and practitioners involving video clips, photos and children's comments. Practitioners have supported children to insert photos, text and sound into easily shared programs such as 2*Create A Story* and *PowerPoint* and then emailed them home.

Of particular relevance at home

Many homes have digital cameras and parents should be encouraged to use these with children and to share some of the images they create with the pre-school.

Tux Paint is well worth looking at as an option for home use. In fact, any freely available software provides the possibility of developing collaborative after-school parent workshop activities where parents can get together with

Imaging movies and graphics

their children to share and develop their skills further (many schools have computer suites that might be borrowed for just this purpose).

Resources

* The digital blue video camera and digital microscopes may be seen on the website www.playdigitalblue.com/home/

* *Tuff Cam* is available from TTS products, including international sales (http://www.tts-group.co.uk).

* *Tux Paint* is a free, drawing program for children ages 3 to 12 (http://www.tuxpaint.org/).

* Drawing for Children is a free drawing and painting application suitable for young children with an intuitive interface and is available from www.cs.uu.nl/people/markov/kids/

Handy helps and tips

The aim in the early years is to promote confidence and competence with a range of technology. In order to ensure that young children have positive and empowering experiences with cameras digital or disposable (video or still) and with digital microscopes practitioners should ensure that:

* The equipment is in working order and set up appropriately
* The equipment is accessible to the child, situated at a low level and within reach
* There are visual instructions clearly displayed
* Children are supported to develop independence in transferring the visual images from the camera or microscope to the computer.

When saving photographs and videos of children on a computer, ensure that you are complying with the specific LEA/setting policy guidance regarding data protection.

When buying a digital camera carefully consider the process involved in transferring the pictures from the camera to the computer. Find one that is intuitive and simple to understand.

Similarly, when purchasing a scanner make sure that it operates simply, with one button on the front panel that produces a scanned image.

Consider investing in re-chargeable batteries and charger units. They are more expensive initially, but could be more cost-effective in the long run.

Handy hints and tips

The RSPB advise that there is no problem with putting a camera in a nestbox or on a feeder. If cameras are stationary they will not disturb the birds. A black and white camera is useful for nestboxes because they will operate during the day without any extra illumination. With a colour webcam light is limited inside the box and you would need some white light. It is possible to use a small bulb or white LED lights. However, if you do so then you must ensure that they are turned off at night-time in order for the birds to recognise night and day. One option is to add some invisible infrared LEDs to record footage of what happens at night.

Programmable toys

In a 'programme', a series of instructions are followed in sequence. A good example is a washing machine. Firstly, a valve or tap opens and the water enters, when it is full the tap closes, and a heater is switched on. When the required temperature is reached the motor begins, and so on.

With moves afoot to replace ICT in the UK National Curriculum for schools with a curriculum subject fiocused upon 'Computer Science', early childhood education may be considered ahead of the game. Programming as a subject is to become more important in years to come and the foundations for this are already being set in many early childhood classrooms.

The use of programmable toys in early years educational settings is based upon the constructionist teaching approach that was first developed by Seymour Papert (1993)[35]. A constructionist approach is underpinned by the idea that learning can happen most effectively when people are actively engaged with doing and making things in the real world. Papert believed that programming could be a valuable activity in supporting young children's emergent mathematical thinking, language development and thinking skills.

There are a large number of programmable toys or controllable robots available for use with young children. In this chapter we mention the Roamer (Valiant technology), the Bee-Bot (TTS), and Pip and Pixie (Swallow Systems) as all of these are routinely used in early years settings. These programmable toys can all be personalised (each to a different extent) and given different identities. Roamers, Pips and Pixies have been used in educational settings with young children for more than 10 years, Bee-Bots are relatively new arrivals to the scene and have only been available for the last few years. Some practitioners have commented that they find that the Bee-Bots are easier for young children to use as they are smaller, lighter, have fewer buttons and are more appealing to look at. Another advantage for use with young

children is that no digit recognition is needed, therefore once children understand that the more times they press the arrow buttons the further the robot moves, they can 'play' with it successfully.

After an initial introduction to the toy, children will generally engage in playful exploratory activity. This initial exploratory activity allows for numerous opportunities for both self-initiated activity, which provide many opportunities for quality adult-child and child-child interactions. This has advantages in terms of getting children to speak, listen to one another's ideas and to develop a shared understandings through discussion and debate of the final sequence of key presses (the program).

Programmable toys

By learning how to input instructions into the keypad of a programmable toy, children will have experiences of making things happen. The keypads allow the input of a direction or number. Successfully engaging in this activity will therefore require the development of understanding about both of direction and number. When playing with these programmable toys children will have the opportunity to engage in activities which allow them to practice the estimation of distance, angle, recognition of numbers, sequencing and logical thinking.

Programmable toys may be utilised to:

- Support creativity by providing for a wide range of possible responses in young children
- Develop the opportunity for children to think and discuss self-initiated problems.
- Allow children the opportunity to think and talk about problems systematically through the process of trying to achieve a set goal with a programmable toy
- Learn by getting things 'wrong', to value the process in addition to achieving the final goal.
- Have what Papert called 'hard fun'.

In planning and programming a programmable toy or robot to act in a particular way children need to see the problem from the perspective of the toy and adopt a body-centred system of reference. What Papert called 'body syntonicity' (Siraj-Blatchford, 2006). Young children can be encouraged to view paths 'from within' rather than 'from outside', or 'from above.' For example, 'turn right' means turn right relative to whatever direction you were heading before, in contrast to 'turn north' which specifies an absolute direction. This means that they can experience working with programmable toys in a way which is compatible with a learner's own experience of moving in the world – it's 'body syntonic.'

Young children love working with programmable toys, getting them to perform simple tasks, but before this, it is useful for them to spend some time being 'programmable' themselves, giving each other instructions to go from place to place, exploring direction, distance and turn as robots. This provides an enjoyable movement activity and also will make the transition to using a programmable toy much smoother.

Many early years teachers have reported the value of developing a strong narrative to provide an underlying rationale for why the programmable toy needs to move in a certain direction. Examples of these include developing a diarama (a three-dimensional scale model) of a local village with prominent shops and buildings, and the need for Jolly Postman Roamer/ Pixie/ Bee-Bot to deliver some letters.

The construction of a fantasy town from blocks, either indoors or outdoors, can also provide a contextualised situation where the optimum motivational level exists for children to instruct a programmable toy to either drive within the walls or to knock them down.

Role play with the programmable toy

Role playing with programmable toys can be an ideal opportunity to assess young children in several areas of learning, including:

- Social skills and working together
- Ability to act out and respond to each other in role
- the ability to create imaginary scenes and scenarios for the programmable toys, and the characters in role
- The ability to program the programmable toy to do exactly what they intended
- Use of language.

Below are some suggestions for role play activities involving programmable toys:

- People who help us – a street cleaner/rubbish collector, a post man/woman, a police car with siren, a fire engine or an ambulance
- Or the programmable toy could be turned into (dressed up as) a character from a book, such as The Hungry Caterpillar, The Jolly Postman etc.
- Turn the programmable toy into a butterfly and visit

Using a programmable toy for purposeful recording (Boogie Bee-Bots)

In a Reception Class in 2009, three pairs of children worked with a teacher and three Bee-Bots. They undertook this Boogie Bee-Bots project over three afternoon sessions.

Session 1: The children were asked to create a dance programme for their Bee-Bots. The children worked in an area which had plenty of space away from the main part of the classroom. The atmosphere was playful and the children enjoyed selecting music from the CDs provided and clearly enjoyed working in pairs getting the Bee-Bot to 'dance'. This involved some discussion (disagreement and resolution) of what made 'good Bee-Bot dancing'. The children came up with some rules such as not going off the dance floor and moving the same way a few times. The teacher then congratulated the children on their Bee-Bot dance ideas. The children used a digital camera to video their Bee-Bot dances.

Session 2: This session began with the children viewing the video clips from the last session. The children were asked if they could remember the instructions they used last time. Some children thought that they could, however when this was tried the dances were clearly different from those in the video. A discussion followed about how we could have remembered these. The children suggested writing the instructions down. It was decided to try this out. The children then worked in pairs to develop and write down new dance routines for the Bee-Bot. This involved a great deal of discussion regarding the best way to do this. The dance routines were placed in a Boogie Bee-Bot Dance Album.

Session 3: This session began by getting the children to choose a dance routine from the Boogie Bee-Bot Dance Album and input the instructions into the Bee-Bot. Once this had been completed the teacher pointed out that all the Bee-Bots were dancing in a different way? Why was that? There was some discussion and a number of responses with the majority of children agreeing that it was because the instructions had been different. The teacher then asked the children how they could make the Bee-bots dance in the same way. At first the children were not sure and some children felt that this was not possible. However one child pointed out that 'If they all have the same instructions, they will all dance the same way!'

A single dance routine was then programmed into all Bee-Bots and the Boogie Bee-Bot dance presented to a group of classmates. Some of the children joined in and danced with the Bee-Bots, managing to follow some but not all of the choreography!

These activities involved lots of discussion, debate, laughter, involvement, co-operation and verbalised thinking.

'flowers' – could put counters on the flowers and collect one each time the butterfly visits the flower

- Children pretend the programmable toy is a school bus. They need to get the bus to travel round a map (or grid) collecting school children.

In addition to programmable toys there is also a wide range of software which promotes a virtual screen version of the real, hands-on experience with these. These include the *Focus on Bee-Bot* software (TTS), *RoamerWorld* (RM), *2go* (2Simple software) *The jelly bean hunt in Trudy's Time* and *Place House* (Riverdeep). There are significant but valueable challenges in moving from the programmable toy to the screen version. The fact that the programmable toy moves on the floor in a horizontal plane and the screen version moves in a vertical plane is in itself a rather challenging activity in terms of spatial thinking. Children will need to cope with a two-dimensional object moving across a computer screen rather than a more tangible three-dimensional object moving across a floor.

Of particular relevance at home

There are lots of ways that adults can support children to develop the knowledge and skills required to access these activities with programmable toys. Many of these do not require access to any ICT equipment, for example:

- Playing games which include counting the number of steps forward, backwards, left or right, can help develop awareness of direction and turn
- Talking about directions when travelling by car, bus, train or walking
- Making a map of a short journey (such as a five min walk) together, including the key landmarks
- Following or planning the feet movements of a dance routine
- Planning out the map of a treasure trail with paper and pencil step-by-step
- Drawing attention to program sequences in the home e.g. the cycles of a washing machine, fan over switching, programmed recording of television.

Programmable toys

'Human robots'

Get children thinking about becoming 'programmable' themselves with the following activity:

Introduce forwards/backwards/left/right and the need for a unit for 'how far'. Then separate turns from distance to travel. Discuss the need for precise language and introduce the need to give instructions in sequence. Ask children to give each other instructions to move around the room, to pick something up, to avoid an obstacle – or any of the floor robot activities below.

Children will need practical experience of seeing and predicting the direction and distance a robot moves, and the amount it turns.

They need time to observe, then to make predictions and to test them. Children will need a lot of support in this – talking about it (with an adult) is a vital part of the process.

It is also possible to access free versions of the Bee-Bot Software and Roamer World for home use.

Resources

- TTS: *Focus on Bee-Bot software* can be downloaded from http://www.bee-bot.co.uk/

- Valiant website: www.valiant-technology.com

- Valiant Roamer free stuff site: http://www.valiant-technology.com/us/pages/roamer_freestuff.php

- Swallow systems: http://www.swallow.co.uk/

[35] Papert S (1993) *The Children's Machine: Rethinking School in the Age of the Computer.* Harvester Wheatsheaf

Interactive Whiteboards (IWBs) and touchscreens

Despite some controversy, Interactive Whiteboards (IWBs) or SMART Boards, are increasingly seen in early childhood educational settings. An IWB is a large display board onto which the computer image is projected, this image can be controlled by touching the surface of the board with a pen or finger. It is therefore possible to write or draw on the surface, and to print the image off or save it electronically. Any computer image can also be annotated, or drawn over with the annotations, additions or amendments saved.

IWB have been identified by some practitioners as a useful pedagogic tool as they exhibit features which promote:

1. Interactivity (they can be used to support active learning rather than any passive reception of information)
2. Collaborative whole class teaching (due to their size)
3. Accessibility (especially for young children and individuals with a visual or physical impairment)
4. Recordability (storing information for re-use and further analysis).

Advocates of IWB technology have suggested that IWBs open up whole new ways of using ICT to support teaching and learning. It is not clear, however, whether this means that there is a change in pedagogical approach as a result of using IWBs, or that tasks within established teaching approaches are technically better supported. The current popularity of IWB technology may in part be due to the well-documented success of whole class plenary sessions associated with the literacy and numeracy initiatives.

Critics of the IWBs question the usefulness of these in early years classrooms and highlight the health and safety problems of encouraging young children to stand in front of a potentially damaging beam. They also point out that similar facilities can be provided at a lower cost using

alternative hardware configurations such as a tablet PC and wireless projector, or by large touch screens.

While there is currently little hard research evidence available to confirm it, many practitioners suggest that touch screens and tablets encourage children's (and especially boys) mark making. Children's mark making is undoubtedly important and should be encouraged wherever possible. When children first realise that marks can be used symbolically to carry meaning, in a similar way to the spoken word, they begin to use marks as tools to make their thinking visible. As they develop their mark making capability, these marks will also support the

Interactive Whiteboards (IWBs) and touchscreens

developing concepts of mathematics and language in relation to their play. Mark making provides a natural and emergent introduction to the world of writing for future literacy and numeracy.

Recent research in classrooms with children aged 3-7 years in Wales[36] suggests that IWBs are routinely being used to support a more didactic form of pedagogy than would be supported by the socio-cultural principles which underpin the new Welsh Foundation Phase. Their application may therefore be undermining the development of more playful learning approaches in the early years.

In this study, although teachers identified their teaching as 'interactive', the classroom observations indicated that in practice the approach was rather different. Indeed, in the majority of the sessions observed, the most common use of the IWB was one where the teacher aimed to impart one specific point of view and take the children through a question and answer routine with the aim of consolidating that point of view.

It may therefore be that whilst the use of the IWB may facilitate greater technological interactivity by allowing access to multi-modal information, and providing a faster and more engaging presentation, they may not presently be being widely used to facilitate greater pedagogical interactivity.[37]

The Foundation Phase practitioners in the study highlighted the potential for developing the use of IWB technology to support:

- The representation and organisation of ideas
- Visualisation and reflection on thinking
- Communication of ideas and collaboration
- Extension and communication of learning to the broader community and documentation of a more divergent form of pedagogical practice.

These four aims could also be supported by touchscreen technology. While IWBs are primarily designed for whole class teaching, touch screens and tablet computers are more appropriate for teacher directed small group work, or for children's independent playful learning. A touchscreen is a computer screen which allows the user to interact directly with the display in the same way as an IWB. It allows the direct interaction with what is displayed on screen with a finger or a stylus, rather than indirectly with a mouse or touchpad. An additional advantage of the touchscreen is that the smaller size means that all areas of the screen can be easily accessible to young children. It also gets over a number of important health and safety considerations regarding the dangers of looking directly at the projector beam which dazzles and flickers, and the potential dangers in some installations of young children climbing on furniture to reach all parts of the board.

There are a number of different IWBs on the market with the two most popular types being the SMART Board and ACTIVboard. These both require users to develop a level of competence with specific software to use the boards proficiently. The software packages are ACTIVprimary and SMART Notebook. These software packages can be installed on most computers, even if they are not connected to an IWB. When using these without an IWB a graphics tablet is useful e.g. an ACTIVtablet.

When working with either an IWB or a touchscreen, activities which best support the development of children's thinking and learning are those where they are:

- Working collaboratively; using the IWB/ touchscreen as a tool for an appropriate purpose
- Engaging in a task controlled by them, rather than one which controls them through programmed learning

Interactive Whiteboards (IWBs) and touchscreens

- Engaging in an activity that demands some 'higher-order' thinking, where answers are not predetermined (i.e. where more than one possible answer exists)
- Supported and guided in their collaboration by an adult or more capable peer.

There are a number of devices which can be attached to a IWB or touchscreen. Appropriate software applied with imaging devices, such as digital cameras and scanners, allow children to select images, change their dimensions, rotate or move them and even make part of the photographs transparent (see **Imaging movies and graphics**). Images can be used to translate the results of activities that children have conducted into an electronic document that can be used for reflection or documentation of this.

The most powerful feature of the IWB is the software which could potentially be used on any platform from a tablet PC to a large interactive touchscreen in the same way. Until recently the ACTIVstudio and ACTIVprimary software was only officially distributed for use with the associated IWBs. Recently however Promethean launched ACTIVinspire, a new version of its software which can be used with or without an IWB.

Of particular relevance at home

Children may already have experience of the type of technological interactivity available on an IWB at home with an iPlayer, an iPhone, a NintendoDS, the WiiTM or a car satellite navigation system. Kiosk touchscreens are also commonly used in libraries, museums, railways and airports. Informal learning situations such as the library and museums now often include the opportunity to experience this type of 'interactive' touch-screen technology. A large number of new applications for children are likely to be developed using these technologies in the next few years. Teachers with iPhones should take a look at applications such as *ABC Oddity* and *iToyBox*.

In terms of children's learning experience the most valuable experience however is the deeper level interaction that comes from sitting with an adult and talking about the experience.

Using the features of the IWB software to reflect on an activity

In a reception/Year 1 classroom children had designed and built shelters in a woodland adjacent to the school with the help of a learning support assistant. Digital photographs of the children's plans and the shelters supported the children in visualising and reflecting upon the work in groups. Comparisons were also made with work undertaken with a different member of staff at a different geographical location. The teacher was able to annotate directly onto the images, recording the children's thoughts and ideas and encouraging the children to do the same, using agreed symbols on additional copies of the images.

These images and the children's ideas scribed by the teacher were used to compile a flipchart of the activity. Unique features of the ACTIVstudio software, such as the ability to annotate, undo and redo, the spotlight and the reveal features were used to good effect to support the discussion and documentation.

Interactive Whiteboards (IWBs) and touchscreens

Handy hints and tips

If you are installing an IWB in an early years setting you need to check that the luminosity of the projector lamp is not above Health and Safety Executive (HSE) guidelines, or install a system that applies the new ultra short throw technology. The positioning of the board and the projector also needs to be carefully considered in the early years classroom. If the projector is too low there may be health and safety issues for the teacher, conversely if the board is too high then the children will be unable to reach very high on the board. If the school decides to use a step or staged area in front of the board this might pose a significant hazard in itself.

Wireless interactive graphics tablets are now being produced by Promethean and Smart Technologies, these allow for the IWB to be controlled from anywhere in the classroom. These are useful in that they remove the need to stand in front of the IWB which can cast a shadow and hide the image being projected. It also partially addresses the health and safety problems of standing in front of a dazzling and flickering beam.

Practitioners should investigate the advantages and disadvantages of both touchscreens and IWBs. It may be that a touchscreen display which does not have the health and safety problems associated with an IWB is more suitable for their purposes.

Resources

- www.prometheanworld.com/uk/
  The Promethean website for information on ACTIVboard™ and the associated software ACTIVstudio and ACTIVprimary.

- www.prometheanplanet.com/
  The Promethean website for ActivInspire. This software combines the functionality of ACTIVstudio and ACTIVprimary. ActivInspire Personal Edition is free and you can use it even if you have another brand of IWB, or no whiteboard at all.

- www.smarttech.com/
  The Smart website for information on SMART Board and the associated software SMART Notebook.

[36] Morgan A (2009) Interactive whiteboards and play in the classroom with children aged 3-7 years. *European Early Childhood Education Research Journal* (in press).

[37] Alexander R (2004) Towards Dialogic Teaching, Rethinking classroom talk. Dialogos.

Appendices

A: ICT policies

Each early years setting should have its own unique ICT policy, the purpose of which is to establish why practitioners and parents consider the use of ICT to be important and of how the setting addresses issues raised by the use of ICT. In your policy please consider the following policy documents and recommended sites:

- e-Safety: Developing whole-school policies http://publications.becta.org.uk/display. cfm?resID=25934&page=1835

- The Byron Review: An independent review looking at the risks to children from exposure to potentially harmful or inappropriate material on the Internet and in video games. http://www.dcsf.gov.uk/ byronreview/

- Child Exploitation and On-line Protection centre http://www.ceop.gov.uk

- The Becta Safeguarding Learners Online Site http://www.becta.org.uk/safeguarding.php

- US National Association for the Education of Young Children (NAEYC) (2012) Position statement on Technology and Interactive Media as Tools in Early Childhood Programs Serving Children from Birth through Age 8: http://www.naeyc.org

B: Health and Safety

Understandably, parents and practitioners have a number of queries and concerns regarding the health and safety issues and other risks, which may be associated with technology routinely used by young children in the home and in formal educational settings. There needs to be careful consideration of how technology impacts upon young children's cognitive, social, emotional and physical development. There are however no large-scale research studies relating the use of ICT to specific health indicators in children[38].

General health awareness relating to ICT use should form part of children's learning about ICT, and should form part of any setting's health and safety policy. Practitioners and young children are not mentioned specifically under any health and safety regulations, or E.U. legislation, with regard to ICT. However, the regulations can be generally interpreted and applied. This section aims to outline the key issues that parents and practitioners should be aware of in order to minimise risk and to promote the safe use of ICT.

Risks to adults relating to computer use are better researched and well-documented, these include repetitive strain injury, carpal tunnel damage, effects upon sight, obesity and the possible risks of radiation exposure from monitors. Particular concerns have been voiced about encouraging extended use of desktop computers by young children. Despite the lack of evidence it seems prudent to limit the time that young children spend at computers to avoid any potential dangers. It is therefore advised that the regular use of any computer application by a child should be relatively short, a maximum duration of no more than 10 to 20 minutes for three-year-olds,

Appendices

extending to no more than 40 minutes by the age of eight. These are only guidelines and clearly, if a child or group of children is totally engaged in an activity and the completion of this requires a longer period at the computer this should be allowed, but it would not be desirable to encourage children to do this regularly.

It is important that, while learning about ICT in their world, children also learn how to manage their own space and select the right tools to use when sitting at a computer. This can be matched to computer use in the world of work. Office workers, for example, are given clear guidance about posture, eye-level, foot rests, arm supports and time to spend on computers. In the same way, children need to become responsible for ensuring that they have a chair of the right height. Cushions can help. Adults of course need to promote this too. They can, for example, ensure that small mice are available for the small hands of children. These can be bought at most reputable computer stores. General health awareness relating to ICT and computer use should form part of children's learning about ICT, and should certainly form part of any setting's health and safety policy.

When using ICT equipment careful consideration should be given to the following:

- Wires and cables for equipment need to be arranged so they can not be tugged, tasted and chewed or tripped over
- Ensuring that all electrical equipment is situated away from fluids (e.g. drinks and the water play area)
- Whether small parts and batteries are well-secured
- Careful use of batteries:
  - ☐ Take care not to mix old and new batteries
  - ☐ Ensure that the batteries used are the type recommended for the item concerned
  - ☐ Never recharge non-rechargeable batteries.

There are particular health and safety considerations relating to the use of projectors in the classroom with young children. Practitioners and children should take care not to look directly at the beam of light from the projector. This means supervising children very carefully to ensure that they do not look directly at the projector.

It is vital that children have the opportunity to engage in vigorous physical activity every day. ICT should and need not be at the expense of outdoor opportunities and experiences which promote the development of essential gross motor skills through running, climbing, jumping, swinging and using wheeled toys. Daily and frequent access to outdoor experiences is essential for all children and their development.

Some ICT applications can encourage playing and being outdoors. Metal detectors have already been mentioned. Identifying ICT in the outdoor environment when out walking or using programmable toys outside can help, but is no substitute for the running and climbing that practitioners should ensure goes on throughout childhood (though it's always possible for some young children to be taking digital pictures of their friends as they run and climb). Where the ICT is integrated with other activities and is used effectively as a tool, for instance in imaginative role play, modelling or painting, children will benefit from greater movement and exercise.

C: Internet safety

Young children, parents and practitioners are using ICT in novel and creative ways. Web 2.0 technologies (which facilitate the online collaboration and sharing by users) allow for the creation of digital content and for communication and collaboration using social software tools. Early years settings are finding it challenging to keep up with both the risks and opportunities presented by these challenges. This section aims to outline some of the resources available to young children, parents and practitioners to assist them in staying safe when online.

1. Consider computer location
With young children, the position of the computer they use is an important consideration. It is recommended that this computer is always situated in an area where young children have access to an adult for discussion whilst using the computer.

2. Consider using kiosk or security software
Consider using kiosk or parental control software, some useful programmes are available free online. Take time to learn how these controls work, most will have options that filter and block inappropriate material. Remember that these programmes all have their limitations and nothing can replace the attention of caring adults who monitor the content of what children in their care are accessing when they are online. Symantec has made onlinefamily.norton.com which has the main features of the best parental control software available free. This software emphasises communication over control.

3. Consider carefully the amount of time children spend online

4. Talk to young children about Internet safety
Explain to children that a computer is a tool and that the Internet is like a giant electronic library full of information. Explain why it's important to be safe online, just as it is important to be safe when you are on a busy street. Talk to them about how, if you are not careful and do not behave safely on the Internet, the computer can be broken. Explain to them that just like if they were on a busy road it is a good idea not to talk to strangers without checking with your teacher or parents first. It is also not a good idea to say yes to new programmes if you do not know where they are from.

5. Use browsers or search engines that do not display inappropriate words or images
Check that they come preloaded with safe web sites and preset word filters. All you need do is review and approve the default web sites and words. Another alternative is to ensure that only predetermined sites are accessed with Internet Explorer 7 by following the below steps:

- Open up Internet Explorer
- Click Tools
- Click Internet Options
- Click on the Content tab
- Underneath Content Advisor, click Enable
- Then click on the tab General
- Under Supervisor Password click Create
- Make your password then click OK
- Click on Approved sites and type in the site you want
- Then click on Apply and finally OK.

D: Digital divide

The 'digital divide' has generally been taken as a reference to the gap between those with effective access to ICT and those without. The term refers to the unequal access of individuals to ICT and to the acquisition of ICT capability. The term 'digital divide' is often associated with the concept of a knowledge divide, as a lack of access to ICT inhibits the ability to access, manage and process information. There is however not a single digital divide but multiple divides between and within countries, between men and women, young and old. Wealth is the major factor underlying these divides. This has implications for both social inclusion and global inequality.

In 1997 the Stevenson Report[39] made a case for the creation of new home-school links through the Internet. Twelve years on children and parents and practitioners are living with inequalities in access to and use of computers and the Internet outside school. There are however examples of initiatives which may illustrate that it can be different. Some early years settings committed to achieving educational opportunity and social justice have developed educational partnerships with parents and have affected home practices. One such project which aimed to increase family involvement with computers encouraged grandparents to sit with their grandchildren and to support them to complete a range of ICT activities.[40]

Initiatives of this kind require resources that are not always available, however there are a number of current initiatives which aim to ensure access for all. The Home Access Project (http://news.becta.org.uk/display.cfm?resID=38386) is intended to bridge the digital divide where currently more than one million children still do not have a computer at home and 35% of families have no access to the Internet. The project will see £300 million spent on providing computers and Internet access to families with the aim of creating a level playing field for learners, where every child has equal access to the Internet at home to assist with their learning.

Appendices

Connectivity is however only the first step in bridging the digital divide. For children, parents and practitioners to benefit from participation in a digital environment, they need support to playfully explore and develop a shared understanding of what ICT might have to offer. In addition to hardware, parents and practitioners need to be provided with the information to make considered and informed choices about how they use the technology together. The development and strengthening of home-school links about and through ICT may prove to be an important vehicle for this information.

Resources (from Adventure and Simulation games chapter)

- Software which support opportunities for collaboration, communication and discussion:
  The Land of Me (http://www.thelandofme.com)
  Soup Toys (http://www.souptoys.com)
  Flying duck (http://www.cgpbooks.co.uk/duckBuilder).

- 2Simple software music toolkit
  (http://www.2simpleshop.com/music/#)
  2Simple products:
  USA (http://www.2simpleusa.com)
  Australia (http://www.2simple.com.au)
  Singapore (http://www.verticalmiles.com).

- Adventure game titles such as:
  Bob the Builder Castle Adventure (PC)
  by Avanquest Software
  Peppa Pig Puddles of Fun (PC)
  by Avanquest Software
  Dora The Explorer World Adventure
  by Avanquest Software.

- The Logical Journey of the Zoombini's by Broderbund.

- Carmen, Sandiego Junior Detective, Diego's Safari Adventure Great Journey by Rebelmind Studios.

- Crystal Rain Forest (Home User) by Sherston.

[39] Stevenson D (1997) *Information and communication technology in UK schools – an independent inquiry.* Independent ICT Schools Commission: London

[40] Kenner C et al (2007) Intergenerational Learning Between Children and Grandparents in East London *Journal of Early Childhood Research* **5**(3): 219-243

Further reading
and useful websites

Further reading

ASA (2002) *Code of practice*, Advertising Standards Authority. (This has now been superceded. For the most recent British Code of Advertising, Sales Promotion and Direct Marketing, see www.asa.org.uk/index.asp?bhcp=1).

Barber, D., Cooper, L., Meeson, G. (2007) *Learning and Teaching with Interactive Whiteboards: Primary and Early Years* (Achieving QTS Practical Handbooks) Learning Matters: London.

Forman, E. (1989) The role of peer interaction in the social construction of mathematical knowledge. *International Journal of Educational Research* **13**: 55–69.

Marsh, J. (2006) Digital Animation in the early years: ICT and Media Education. In: Whitebread D,Hayes M, eds *ICT in the Early Years*. Open University Press: London.

Papert, S. (1993) *The Children's Machine: Rethinking School in the Age of the Computer*. Harvester Wheatsheaf.

Siraj-Blatchford, I., Siraj-Blatchford, J. (2000) *More than Computers: Information and Communications Technology in the Early Years*. Early Education (The British Association for Early Childhood Education): London.

Siraj-Blatchford, J. (2003) *Developing new technologies for young children*. Trentham Books: Stoke-on-Trent.

Siraj-Blatchford, J., Siraj-Blatchford, I. (2002) IBM KidSmart early learning programme: UK Evaluation Report – Phase 1 (2000–2001). IBM: London.

Siraj-Blatchford, J., Whitebread, D. (2003) *Supporting information and communications technology education in early childhood*. Open University Press: Buckingham.

Stevenson, D. (1997) *Information and communication technology in UK schools—an independent inquiry*. Independent ICT Schools Commission: London.

Useful websites

The following sites are well worth a browse. But any programs applied, downloaded or purchased should be evaluated in light of the principles outlined in the introduction.

http://ictearlyyears.e2bn.org/
http://www.327matters.org/download.htm
http://tuxpaint.org/
http://www.bbc.co.uk/cbeebies/big-and-small/games/
http://www.sesamestreet.org/games
http://pbskids.org/superwhy/
http://www.kbears.com/playmusic/keyboard.html
http://pbskids.org/mamamirabelle/whereintheworld.html
http://www.madeinme.co.uk
http://www.nationalgeographic.com/kids/
http://www.peterrabbit.com/
http://pbskids.org/
http://www.hitentertainment.com/thomasandfriends/uk/
http://www.bbc.co.uk/cbbc/games/
http://www.enchantedlearning.com/categories/preschool.shtml
http://www.sustainabilityed.org/how/play_the_game/play.html
http://pagesperso-orange.fr/jeux.lulu/english.htm
http://www.uptoten.com/kids/uptoten-home.html
http://www.bbc.co.uk/cbeebies/bigandsmall/fun/
http://www.sesamestreet.org/games
http://www.cgpbooks.co.uk/duckBuilder
http://pbskids.org/superwhy/
http://earth.google.com/
http://www.playthinklearn.org

Glossary of terms

Android: An increasingly popular operating system for smartphones.

App: An 'application' is a software program. While the shortened term 'app' was used exclusively in the past in the context of smart phones and tablets it is increasingly being applied in the context of desktop and laptop computer programs.

Bandwidth: A measure of data (information) transmission, the broader the bandwidth, the quicker the information can be transmitted. Usually measured in kilobits per second (Kbps) or megabits per second (Mbps).

Broadband: A class of transmission system which allows large amounts of data (information) to be transferred at high speed. Any Internet connection that is faster than 128Kbps has been considered as 'broadband', home cable modem service now provide up to 3Mbps.

Browser: A programme that allows you to search the World Wide Web (e.g. Internet Explorer/Netscape/Mozilla).

Firewall: An Internet gateway that limits access e.g. protecting the user from viruses and pornography. Internet 'filters' are available to protect children, but for more effective protection see BrowserLock (http:\\www.browserlock.com).

Graphics tablet: Provides a digital pencil or stylus for computer drawing (or tracing).

Interactive Whiteboard: A large wall or board mounted display which is connected to a computer and projector that allows user interaction via a pen or finger.

Internet: A worldwide association of interconnected networks of connected computers. This network provides for the transfer of files, remote login, electronic mail, news, search and other services.

Internet filtering: Software that gives you the ability to control content displayed, block websites and set up passwords to protect children/adults from pornography, chat sites etc. Popular products include *ContentProtect NetNanny* and *CyberSitter*. See also Firewall.

ISP (Internet Service Provider): A company that supplies Internet services to its customers. An ISP account provides a username and a password which allow users to login and access the Internet network or a specific service on the Internet, such as an email box.

JPG (or jpeg): Format for compressing images, suitable for photographs and for very detailed drawings. Even though this is the ideal format for storing and communication photographs on the Internet, it may produce images whose quality is lower than the original.

Operating System (OS): The main software program that runs a computer or smartphone. The most common operating systems are now Windows (95, 98, 2000, XP, Vista), Mac OS (8, 9, 10, X), Android, LINUX and UNIX.

Server: This is a computer that is set up to 'serve' web pages on the Internet.

Scanner: A device for capturing a digital image of a drawing or picture.

SMART Board: A large whiteboard that uses touch technology for detecting user input, the SMART Board also has 4 digital writing utensils that use digital ink.

Smartphone: All mobile telephones are computerised but 'smartphones' are mobile telephones with wireless (radio) Internet access, and the capability of running Apps (see above).

Software: Computer programmes (often contrasted with 'hardware' – the physical equipment of a computer system and/or 'liveware' – the human user/operators of computer systems, who are sometimes considered to merely complement the hardware and software!)

Sustained shared thinking: An effective pedagogic interaction, where two or more individuals 'work together' in an intellectual way to solve a problem, clarify a concept, evaluate activities or extend a narrative.

Tablet (or Tablet PC): A handheld computer with a touch-sensitive screen.

Touch screen: A display that can detect the presence and location of a touch of a finger within the display area.

Universal Resource Locator (URL): The 'address' of a website. They usually (but not always) begin with http://www.

Virus: A software programme, usually downloaded from the Internet, that infiltrates a computer, making something happen that you would rather not (e.g. loss of data).

Web/World Wide Web/WWW: Another name for the Internet.

WebCam: A small video camera that usually plugs into the USB socket of your PC. While designed primarily for use on the Internet, webcams provide an inexpensive and versatile means of recording and playing back video for a variety of purposes.

Wi-Fi: a technology that allows a computer, smartphone or peripheral device to connect to other devices and/or the Internet wirelessly (using radio waves). For most practical purposes the term WiFi can also be used synonymously with the term ' wireless local area network' (WLAN).

Website: Pages posted on the Internet. These pages are accessed using an URL and may be maintained by an ISP or other individual or institution with the appropriate 'server'.

Webmail: Electronic email server, which can be accessed through a Browser.

Index